UNASHAMED: BROKEN TO HEAL

Faith In The Midst of the Mess

SAMONE BATAIR

ISBN: 978-1-66783-216-6 (softcover)
ISBN: 978-1-66783-217-3 (eBook)

*I can do all things through Christ
who strengthens me.*

—PHILIPPIANS 4:13

Table of Contents

DEDICATION

To My Lord and Savior Jesus Christ, for allowing me the gift to walk in purpose, always beyond measure, merciful, graceful, forgiving, and loving, for His wisdom, faithfulness, and strength. For being my keeper and best friend, never turning His back on me, and making the paths of my way straight. For salvation, transformation and breaking generational curses. To my four boys God was so gracious and generous to allow me to have. For the motivation from my children whose constant support and presence pushed me forward to pursue my dreams. To the life trials that turned into lessons then triumphs, from tests into testimonies. To the storms that tried to take me over, and for which I am thankful that God sustained me throughout. To the girls and women who feel broken and need that extra encouragement through life, know that you are never alone.

Prayer

Lord Jesus, please help guide the words I write in this book to be an anointed invitation and opportunity to the reader to break the strongholds of chains that bind them, that my words will help them break free of all bondage. Please forgive us for our sins and the times we cast you away when we were in darkness. Strengthen our minds with wisdom to allow our feet to walk in your light, for your glory, honor, and praise. Thank you, Lord, for all you have done and thank you in advance for everything you are getting ready to do. Help us to understand that you do not allow storms to come into our lives without leaving your love and grace behind them. Allow us to understand for every season there is a purpose and for every person

1

there is a season. Help us to be secure and at peace in knowing that everyone and everything within and around us is not meant to stay past their allotted time. Please help guide us to the path you have created and ordained specifically to every one of us and help us accept what crosses our path as part of your divine plan. Lead us so we can do the work that needs to be done, to be door keepers and add to your kingdom. Help us to heal the wounds known and unknown to us and move past closed doors. Help us not to go back to the negative habits, characteristics, and individuals that have kept us in captivity and drawn us away from you, Lord Jesus. Let every chain be broken in the blood of Jesus. Help us to see the fruitfulness of your spirit and presence. We thank you in advance for deliverance and having your way with our lives. For keeping us when we did not want to be kept and keeping your word that the destiny you created for us would be fulfilled. We thank you and love you. In your precious name we pray, and we receive that it is done, In Jesus' Name, Amen.

INTRODUCTION

When I first decided to put forth the effort to write this book, something rooted in me that I always wanted to do, I was in the most spiritual transitional point in my life, but I knew that if nothing else—even with my own brokenness, hurt, fears, doubts, pain, and tribulations, I wanted to make an impact. Even if just one person reads this book, whom I help lead to Christ, renewing their spirit and ability, my mission will be complete. My goal for this book is to have an impact by influencing readers to a positive surrender into salvation, to be encouraged and strengthened.

From the first time I learned how to hold a writing utensil to paper, it was always my passion to write. Writing for me has always been the best route of expression. As a little girl, I would sit in the corner of a room and write poems and short stories with colored gel pens, as I had many thoughts and experiences flowing through me that I wanted to release into the universe. I prayed about where I should start and what type of book I should write. In fact, the first book I started to write was in the genre of romantic fiction, but I could hear God telling me, "No that's not it, but you will write a book." I knew that I wanted to be passionate about what I was writing, and although romantic love is a passion, it was more moving in my heart to be a resource to encourage others to come to Christ, to help bring healing and transform lives.

First, I want to embrace you with a hug wherever you are. You did not pick up this book by mistake. I want to let you know that you are my friend, sister, my mother, my aunt, my niece, even my grandmother. I love you! Sometimes it is hard to love yourself because you may feel that you are not deserving of love or have been shown that no one does actually love you. *Know that I do.* I mean that with everything in my soul. For I, too, know the cries and the joys. I know some days can be good and on others, you can barely find the strength to make it through. I know what it's like to feel so broken down and ready to give up on life because it seems to demand too much of you. I know there are days when you are even mad at God and feel He is nowhere to be found. Or you may have had the thought that you have messed up in life so badly and too many times. You may think it is too late, and it is over for you. One day you have the feeling that you can conquer the world and the next day you're wondering where you went wrong, replaying regrets, even obsessing over sins that you have committed and you're thinking that maybe you deserve punishment and that's what you're experiencing right now.

Ultimately, more than anything, you crave to be the best version of yourself, to love yourself, to feel loved and genuinely needed, and to know that you matter wholeheartedly. The reality is it's God's love that you need. The most important person to heal is yourself and God wants that for you. It is so easy to become a victim, getting caught in what we lost, or in what may have happened to us, and all that we feel we don't have. We can easily miss the blessing in the circumstances. But your "right now" is not your forever.

When you begin to thirst for Christ, trust God, follow God, and put Him first in all that you do, everything else will flow from that. You will find yourself yearning for a closer relationship with God that is true and intimate as well as yearning with the desire to walk only in His ways and purpose for your life. You will find yourself not settling for people and things that do not elevate your being and bring you to higher, more fulfilling grounds. You will find yourself content and at peace with being alone instead of wasting your time and energy in the wrong relationships and situations with the wrong people and influences. You will find yourself no longer compromising your worth and chasing after your dreams, the ones that you thought had died, or you lacked the courage to go after. You may have felt you were not good enough to pursue them. You will find yourself wanting to live healthy and take better care of yourself. I know it sounds like unicorns and rainbows, but I can guarantee the work and the walk is worth it. Jesus Christ is with you holding your hand each and every step of the way.

CHAPTER 1—ALREADY ON THE WINNING SIDE

I t is ultimately within us to know better. It is up to us if we want to do and be better, even if your childhood was not ideal and has been phased with trauma. Or if you have lacked love, affection, guidance, have been betrayed in the parental roles that were set in front of you, or by others who were supposed to love you but instead broke your confidence or your spirit. You may have grown up in poverty or in a neighborhood of negative influences, violence, and drugs. You may have been or are battling some form of addictions. There comes a point in your life where you must take charge and accountability to be the person you desire to be and not allow your past encounters, choices, or circumstances to dictate where your life is headed and who you are going to be.

Even to the day of the writing of this book my mother and I have not spoken to each other in over fifteen years, and I have not seen her since I was put out of her house on my eighteenth birthday, on a frigid Minnesota winter day, seven months pregnant with my first child. The ground was covered in ice and ten inches of snow that accumulated over the last few days. As I was upstairs gathering all that I owned, my mother sat downstairs silenced in her bedroom. I desperately waited for the moment she would have a change of heart and tell me not to leave. That moment would not come. I can still see myself moving my belongings out of her home in the black garbage bags I dragged to the bus stop four blocks away, exhausting my strength, taking short breaks as the cold pierced my frail pregnant body. I remember my mother's voice stabbing like a knife thrust, "I can't wait until you are eighteen and get out my house," echoed by bursts of freezing wind as I hauled the fatigue of my body, my child, and the little that I took with me. I was thankful for the moment when the wheels of the bus pulled up to a screeching halt and I was able to embrace a hint of warmth.

We never had a true mother/daughter relationship. The one person who was supposed to be my biggest cheerleader and protector had tried to put me in positions that were meant to fail. The one place called home that should have been a haven for me, I felt was my hell on earth. Dehumanized by her attempt to belittle me, I had never been called by my name, and I was always referenced as "girl." I lived in an environment where food would be cooked then quickly stashed away so that I could not eat. As a little girl I never had a bedroom or bedroom set glamorized in girly colors, let alone a bed to call my own. The arduous relationship and treatment could have been used as an excuse to be the reason not to do better, to take drugs, sell my body, go in and out of the prison system, or even not to be a good mother to my own children. In the beginning I allowed the trauma from that relationship to trigger me and dictate my earlier choices in life.

For several years, I despised holidays such as Thanksgiving, Christmas, and Mother's Day in particular. I did not enjoy such holidays because they represented for me family, love, laughing, hugs, togetherness, and appreciation for one another, something that was not embraced by my mother or her side of the family. In my first few years of my own motherhood, I didn't appreciate myself on Mother's Days, even after having children of my own, because I could not personally relate to what it felt like to have a mother. Instead I would feel deeply-rooted envy when I saw other people who were able to enjoy their families, people looking forward to making lifelong memories where daughters reached out for reciprocating love from their mothers. However, I knew somewhere, in the long run, it was crucial for me to decide to *disallow* my own broken relationship with my mother and my own unfortunate circumstances to determine the rest of my life as an individual, my future relationships, and most importantly, the relationships I needed to have with Jesus and with my own children.

Think back and imagine yourself as a child again. You are on the playground with other children, and you notice there is another child off to the side playing all alone. You decide to approach this child to play but she just pushes you down to the ground and walks away. The next day you see this same child again. Your thinking is set to give the benefit of the doubt, and you decide you will try again to see if this child wants to play with you today. The child leans forward and again gives you a shove and walks away. You pick yourself up from those assaults, but I can guarantee on that third day when you see this same child at the playground your instincts will tell you to avoid this child who made you feel badly about trying to engage with her. Therefore the situation has set the tone for you to make better choices due to what you have encountered. In essence, it is about treating yourself better, knowing your own self-worth, as well as setting the tone for the future of how much you will willingly take from someone who treats you badly and to what extent you will place limits on what you choose to engage in. Now a lesson has been learned, because when you know better, you do better. You are thinking you should have known better after the first time, or at least the second time you were pushed down in the dirty leaves. Right? Or why did you ignore the signs and signals that maybe this child wasn't as approachable to play with as you thought?

When I began writing this book, I questioned myself and became discouraged multiple times during my writing. I worried that my material wouldn't be considered "structured" in the way that would be acceptable in a book-writing world, despite all the tears that had dropped onto the drafts I had written. I read articles of a dos and don'ts within a self-help memoir, genres that were considered best-selling, because I wanted this book to reach people and knew that some may feel that in the content of this book my thoughts were all over the place, or that I over-emphasized the major message, since at the heart of the book, the main objective is the same. *What is meant to break you has value, holds healing and elevation if you allow it, no matter what you are up against.*

Within this book we will uncover identity traits which can lead you into situations and/or relationships not best suited for you. We will whisk through the qualities the person who is called to walk this life with you will hold. We will look at phases during the process of self-healing. I will also nakedly and unashamedly touch on the background of my early relationships, my healing journey, to the point of my acceptance of the best I knew I deserved, allowing Jesus Christ to come fully into my heart and every part of my being.

I have come as a messenger for the betterment of your life to extend a branch of healing, and I mention lastly, but most importantly, the necessity that we must always follow Christ. This is the reason I am unashamed. I am unashamed of my delivery and unashamed of my journey, no matter how it is sliced and diced. Whether it is deemed traditional or not, I have faith this book will land in the hands of those who need it. This is what God directed in my heart, an avenue for me to walk, helping someone else who needs a renavigation of their GPS, which I call God's Purposed Soul. I will take you through personal walks of brokenness to healing in hopes that I can encourage you within all the areas of your life. I invite you to accept renewal, not to become stuck in your circumstances and become instead, the best version of yourself, embracing all you are worthy of, which is the absolute 100% very best! That is what God wants for you. I say "invitation" because ultimately, it is up to you to decide to accept. No one else can walk the journey for you. You may not be where you want to be in life right now but do not let that devalue the journey where you are at this time. It is like being at the beach, you cannot lie in the sand and be in the water at the same time. In life, you can either choose to sink or swim. Look down at your shoelaces every now and again and make sure they are still laced for the race. There will be times where they will loosen but you can tighten them again, not allowing them to become unlaced and trip you. Think of those shoelaces as your life. How will your shoelaces be taken care of? You are equipped to run the race!

I want everyone, both male and female, to be able to read this book, as there are men who are stuck, broken and need healing as well. I believe people of either gender can take something away from it, but my focus is for My Queens. We, as women, are the foundation of this world and it is so imperative for us to stand strong and bold, overcoming the many obstacles that life can throw our way in the attempt to take us down. Many of us are parents and caregivers and if we do not hold it together then that foundation begins to be chipped away and cause the domino effect of our parenting, our jobs, our dreams, our sense of self and the overall ability to move forward is at stake. My hope and goal for you is that my stumbling blocks become your stepping-stones.

I, myself, did not have a support system to lean on, or cheer me on while standing behind me. I made the decision myself to improve my life with discipline and courage. That decision starts with YOU! My purpose is to give insight, motivation, encouragement, and influence, as life is not always easy. I took a lot of detours because I lacked wisdom. By the grace of God, I learned through experiences which are now my testimonies to you because I did not know I was a child of the Highest Father, who cared about every detail of my being. Not personally in-tune of my worth, and I engaged in unhealthy relationships and crossed unhealthy boundaries.

I thought I could sweep under the rug, events that were traumatizing to me and just move forward in life. The most life-changing event of all was coming to the realization that I needed Christ in the center of my life. You too can save yourself energy

11

from a lot of extended trauma and difficulties by knowing who God is and that He stands behind you despite where you have come from or in what circumstances you may have begun. *ALL THE WAY NO MATTER WHAT!*

Think of it like the study sheets your teacher would give to you to review before a test so that you would not have to dance around a problem to find the solution. If nobody else is rooting for you, know that I am genuinely rooting for you. I have been in these same shadows you are in and have been in. When you feel alone, and the weight of the world seems to be on your shoulders. When you feel rebellious because life seems not to work out in your favor. If you feel that no one on Earth understands, cares, and/or loves you— know that I do. And God cares and loves you that much more. You are blessed to be a child of The Highest Father, the Alpha, and the Omega. You are given the ability to heal. Be bold, be confident, dream big and love yourself. It matters to me that you come out on the winning side. *You will come out on the winning side!*

Chapter 2—A Trapped Little Girl

Growing up, I suffered from low self-esteem. Any level of low on the self-esteem spectrum that anyone could possibly have, I seem to have had it. I was my own worst enemy and very critical of myself. Physically, it seemed I was always the darkest, tallest girl. My teeth were jagged, and I did not have long natural hair tresses flowing from my scalp down my back. Neither did I wear what was considered the latest fashion. I was never in the category of being one of the smartest or most popular in school. I was shy, a quiet loner, and considered myself "socially awkward," envious of the extroverts that seemed to surround me. I liked to have some social interactions, then again, preferred to be left alone at the same time. It appeared to me that the talent of everyone around me came to them so naturally. Add to that, the factor that I did not come from a home where "I love you" was spoken. Much less shouted. And hugs were not warmly embraced. Family functions were not memorable or very functionable. Laughter did not fill the rooms and positive affirmations were non-existent.

I was not raised by my biological father, a man named Joey who was of Spanish descent, whom I called "dad." My mother had been in an off and on again type of relationship since they were teenagers, growing up in the projects next door to each other in Illinois. They eventually decided to settle In Minnesota and had married. He was the biological father of my two sisters after me, but he was the only man I knew as a father until the age of 12. When I look back, during those years, my father would pop in and out of the picture, always coming back in the wee hours of the early morning awakening us from our deep sleep bearing gifts for us as if it was Christmas morning.

Several years later the marriage dissolved; I was never privy to the specifics. I do remember the weeks leading up to my father leaving. He let my sister's and I know. The day of his departure became a reality on a Friday, a sunny humid day in the month of June. My sisters and I sat on the deck eating popsicles that were melting faster than we could lick them away. As he loaded his baby blue pickup truck, we could read engraved on the back window "widow maker." Heavy tears began flowing from our faces. We hugged and said our final goodbyes, and he said to us, "I love you girls and I will call you as soon as I get to Illinois." We watched him drive away until we could see him no longer and the remnant of exhaust faded away. That was my first encounter with heartbreak. At 12 years old I could not comprehend how to deal with the heaviness I felt in my heart, and my mother did not attempt to console or offer any explanations. Within a year of his leaving, divorce was finalized. Although she would quickly remarry, the man she chose to wed did not help to bridge the gap between the relationship I had with my mother or with the family as a whole.

Starting at the age of 10, I had my first thoughts of suicide, along with a few artificial attempts such as cutting myself because I was feeling that I wanted to die and felt I was not worthy of living. I remember locking myself in the bathroom with a utility knife. Red eyes, face puffy, from hard crying that fell like a waterfall from my eyes. I ran the blade from the inner part of my elbow to the end of my wrists drawing blood. But the pain of my cuts felt numb. I did not like myself as a person and felt I was in the wrong line at birth when God was handing out looks, gifts, and families. I did not have any friends, I did not have family I was close to, and I felt I was left without any parental figures to whom I was dear to their heart. I did not know my place in the world or who I was. I did not feel childlike and I was not shown love or that my very existence and well-being mattered to anyone because no one was ever there to rescue me when I was drowning. My mom never paid me any attention, not so as even asking how my day was or if there was anything that I needed. No hugs, no words of affection, or family game nights or dinner around a dinner table. There were never conversations. A home filled with quietness, as a room of students taking a test. Coming home after school I was not offered help with homework. I would simply come home and go to my empty room, where a curtain was over the window to keep the neighbors from looking in, and my makeshift bed, which was a pile of blankets. My clothes, folded in a neat pile in the corner of the room. It was not of importance to know if I had any friends, or to know the fact that I played alone on the playground during recess. Not to mention the cringy moments in class when the teacher would say, "find a partner." I despised those type of in-class assignments. I felt that I was just not good enough across the board, and there were no acts of reassurance or models to offset or discourage my frame of thinking.

There were times as a child I would plead with my mother that if she did not want me, to give me up for adoption to someone who would love me. Why allow me to suffer? I did not ask to be brought into this world, let alone be born to her. One day I came to her bedroom as she was lying across the bed watching TV and asked why she did not like me? Why we did not have a mother and daughter relationship where we would go shopping or have talks? Stone cold as an iceberg, she did not bat an eye to my questions, or move a muscle in her body as she stared blankly at the TV as if I was not in the room. I left the room crying, feeling pitiful and mad with God.

I was molded at an early age that it was up to me to look out for me. When I was thirteen-years old, I became ill with a sore throat. For a few days I thought I had a flu and tried to nurse myself back to health by drinking tea, taking cold medicine, and swallowing cough drops to no avail. I remember vividly it was a Sunday afternoon, because we had gone to church that day and my throat had become so inflamed, I could barely swallow. I felt as if my throat was literally on fire. I rolled around on my cot of blankets on the floor in agony. To deaf ears, I pleaded for my mother to take me to the hospital. The pain became so unbearable I could hardly breathe and had no choice but to call 911. When the paramedics arrived, my mother still denied me medical care, so the police were brought into my medical situation. She had to be threatened to be taken to jail for child neglect in order for me to go to the hospital. It turned out I had strep throat. My mother who was very defiant and stubborn, her eyes pierced with hatred towards me. She never once came into the back room to check on me or ask me how I was feeling, before, during or after. I remember the police officer sticking around from beginning to end to make sure that I was given the treatment I needed, and that my prescription was filled before leaving the hospital.

At the time I was ignorant of the fact that if left untreated, strep could cause other serious medical conditions. I thought maybe that is what my mother wanted for me. Again, I began thinking it was best that I was just not alive— period. If I didn't exist, then my mother's problem with me would be solved and both of us would be better off. If I no longer were on this earth, I would not feel the emotional pain that I felt, and all loneliness and misery would end. My brother Kenneth who was two years older than me was on a home visit that weekend and sat with me in the hospital room. When he was 12, he was taken out of our mother's home to foster care. When our parents bought a house, we moved from Minneapolis to a smaller city suburb across town thirty minutes away. At our new school my brother and I began to confide in the school counselor whose name was Nell. She had big red hair, wore big black frame glasses, and she always covered herself with long necklaces and lots of bracelets that jangled with any movement of her body. Her office was filled with bright colors, candy jars, with toys and stuffed animals that decorated the room allowing a child to feel welcomed. Nell became a therapist for me to be open about how I felt, in the way I could not with my parents. Nell would embrace me with warm hugs, a gentle smile and kind words soothing my heart in a soft tone. I would believe it was the same for my brother because he would go to her office as well. I am not sure of everything Kenneth spoke about with Nell, but when he would be physically reprimanded at home, he would be sure to tell her. One night we were supposed to be in bed, however we were playfully jumping around, and Dad came upstairs and hit him with a stick. Aimlessly swinging without turning on the light, Kenneth was struck across his face, under his eye, as we were warned again. "There is no more goofing around; it is time to go to sleep."

February, Valentine's Day, was our parents' wedding anniversary and that year they decided to go to Puerto Rico for a week because that was where Dad was born. Our maternal grandmother, traveled from Indiana to watch us and while she was there, Kenneth chose to do what he wanted to do. He stayed at his friend's house without permission, money that was left in a drawer in the bedroom for our grandmother in case of an emergency was partially taken, and when the deacon from church came to pick us up for service Kenneth was not anywhere to be found. When my parents came back and received the report, he received a spanking. I remember it clearly as the blue sky. It was a Monday and while we were getting ready for school that is when our mom confronted Kenneth. My mom whipped him with a belt and my dad held him. Although I knew I did not do anything to be next, in fear I ran to the basement, getting dressed underneath the stairs as I heard my brother cry out with each strike from the belt. When my brother and I walked to school that cloudy, misty morning I remember asking him, "Are you ok?" With no response he just walked as tears fell from his eyes.

By the end of the school day Nell had brought me out of class early to let me know that my brother would not be coming home with me. Feeling confused by what she meant, I sat in a chair at the round table in the center of her room, and not the orange bean bag chair I would usually rest myself in. I remember her telling me not to tell my parents when I got home but to wait a while. I walked home slowly, bouncing back and forth in my mind to tell my parents about Kenneth or to wait as Nell instructed me. I decided to tell my dad as soon as I walked in the door. He was watching TV, reclined in his grey lazy boy off work due to a recent back surgery procedure. He called my mom who came home from work and the next thing I knew we were at the police station. It turns out all those months Kenneth and I were talking to Nell about home, she was documenting, building a child protection case. The whipping that he received, with welp marks was, apparently, the final straw to break the camel's back. Later my mother would lose her parental rights to my brother who then became a ward of the state, never to permanently reside in her home again as a minor.

When I was 11 years old, just a few weeks after Kenneth left, I was placed for a short period of time into the same foster home as my brother for an "out of home evaluation," as they called it. I can recall an incident when I was in the second grade and was yelling because my brother would not stop messing with me—ordinary sibling play rivalry—and my mother who was opening her mail with a letter opener became overly annoyed and held the letter opener to my throat, threatening to kill me. Although this incident occurred a few months before I met Nell, in confidence I told her about it, and brought the letter opener to her, never to see it again.

Growing up I was whipped with an extension cord and a belt, hit with hot spoons and hangers, or anything else that could be quickly thrown across the room. Sometimes as punishment, my brother and I would have to stand against the wall with our hands in the air for long periods of time. All the blood rushed out our fingertips to the end of our arms, numbing the shoulders and at any time feeling as if parts of us would just fall off. That punishment was usually at the direction of Joey, whom Kenneth, also at one point called, "dad," because he did not know who his biological father was either. This punishment was enough to be called "child abuse" by the county.

The evening the social worker who was assigned to our case and a police officer came to the house to take me to foster care, I remember my mother just stood at the back door on the deck with her hands crossed against her chest. No hugs, no cries, no goodbyes, no words of comfort like, "it will be ok." I look back at it now and think with empathy how helpless she must have felt, but my mother was never the one to show any type of humanly emotion, affection, or care. Always stoned face, or as contemporary slang might call it now, "resting(you fill in the blank)face." Just completely emotionless. My dad hugged me as he handed me a bag of a few clothes he had packed and said, "everything is going to be ok." I walked to where the officer and social worker were standing outside their cars, with my head held down, clutching my bag on my side for comfort, internally shaking as I did not know what to expect next. By the same token, I was curious to know who I was going to live with since my brother had not returned and maybe living elsewhere would be better than the home we knew, for the both of us. The foster dad, Mr. Jackson, who was on the meek and quieter side, took all the foster children to school every morning and prepared our meals, but the foster mom, Mrs. Jackson, was terribly mean to me. Not too long after arriving, she snapped at me for crying about going home. I always cried because if I was still going to experience someone not treating me well, I would have rather been where I was used to.

Standing in the foyer, with my back against the wall, she waved her pointed finger in my face, breathe smelling of a stale ashtray and shouted. "You are crying and want to go back home to parents who do not care about you or take care of you. If your home was good to you, then your brother and you would not be in my house, would you?" The two months that I was in the foster home, I cried the whole time. Because of the added psychological changes, I started to wet the bed every night and apparently that also irritated Mrs. Jackson. When I was in the hospital being treated for strep throat, reminded me of that day, three years prior when I was sent to that foster care with The Jacksons. I can still see my mother's wooden demeanor, her perpetual, expressionless frown when she looked at me, as if I had asked to get strep throat.

I was not sure if the hotline to God was busy or maybe I was not eligible to allow God to hear me. The painful situation just did not make sense to me. Jesus is so forgiving and loving; he sat with and healed sinners, yet my own mother condemned me. Still, this was a woman who kept us in church for Sunday school, Sunday service, service after Sunday service, Bible study, vacation bible school, who all the while did not face her own demons and her own childhood trauma and relationship with her parents and others who she felt failed her. This is an example of what happens when we do not deal with the issues, we have faced that have hurt us or have affected us in a negative light. We ignore the piles in the closet and those piles get passed down from generation to generation. When the only time the closet is open, is when it is time to stuff more trauma into it. My grandmother was not a "typical" affectionate grandparent; therefore her children did not receive motherly affection, linking to why everyone on my mom's side of family finds expressing love a deadly disease.

My mother was the ninth child of twelve and I am sure it was a difficult task for my grandparents to spread equal quality time with each child. I never knew my grandfather, he was not talked about, I just know that he died when I was a toddler of some sort of blood disease. I know some may be wondering what I contributed to the demise of a mother/daughter relationship. I was not completely innocent growing up, and I am in no way excusing my actions but they were typical, immature, and rebellious behaviors. Once my dad left the home and walked away from the family, I was fighting to get my mother's attention and love even if it was not in the most positive light. There were times that I did steal money from my mother. One time I stole money from her ATM card so that I could go to the toy store and buy Barbies. I did not know how to catch the bus, so I caught cabs. I didn't know any better; I was about twelve and I kept going to the ATM to try to get $5.00 but it kept only delivering $50.00. Going back a few times trying to get that $5.00, thinking I was doing it wrong, allowed the $50.00 withdrawal increments to add up. When our Dad decided to leave the family, our mom worked nights and I would write out checks to have pizzas delivered for me and my sisters not knowing that the checks that were written were sent back in the mail with the monthly bank statement each month, which was, of course, how my mother found out about my little scheme.

Another time I took money so that I could buy her a white 3-piece suit for her birthday as a surprise, claiming it was from someone else. She had always mentioned she wanted a white suit to wear because the 3rd Sunday of each month was "Women's Day" at church. I also wanted to try to do something to right the wrongs she felt I ever did to her because I craved love and affection from her and wanted her to see me. I also wanted to do anything to make her smile. I never remember my mother smiling. I was a child and just didn't know that taking that money would cause her to be late with the mortgage payment as she claimed. She looked at me as a thief and a liar. I was becoming a teenage girl on my own and alone with no guidance.

There were many times I did not come home to avoid arguing with her, which led to a few physical altercations between us with me challenging her authority. I do not condone being physical with your parents as the Bible tells us to honor our mother and father. The memories of my transgressions are not something I am proud of. And I have repented. My mother always accused me of behavior that I did not engage in, but she could only use her imagination of what I might be doing out all night since we did not have a bridge of communication. But I was not out doing drugs, drinking alcohol or being sexually promiscuous with men as she had always assumed. Although I did experiment with alcohol at thirteen, I did not smoke weed until I was seventeen or eighteen years old. When she and Joey, the father I had known, separated, I think she felt at one point that I was choosing his side and I did at the time because he was the only one of the two of them that ever showed any type of love and care for me. I even began to wonder as I became older if she felt betrayed by Kenneth and me for talking with Nell. At times I would feel guilty that some circumstances may have been a bit different if we had never confided in Nell, although knowing the characteristics of our mother, probably not so much.

Were these small rebellions enough to throw a daughter into the pit of never and forever? I understand now it had to be much deeper than that. Were my actions bad enough to cut off the chance of having a relationship with her grandchildren? Apparently so. And when my own children grew older, they questioned why they didn't have a grandmother. I had to learn to bridge the gap of what my children were not experiencing regarding "family units" even when certain family members were alive and well. While teaching my children, I also had to learn myself to accept that every family dynamic is different and let go of what society thought to be a "normal" family, to learn to be content with having those around who feel love and concern mutually, even when those who are considered family are not blood related. I always enjoyed watching crime tv and was amazed to see that there are mass murderers whose mothers stuck by them, standing by their child's side even with every obvious evidence of their guilt. I could not wrap my mind around it, but I began to accept the relationship for what it was and was not, possibly what it may never be.

So many times, I questioned God, Why Me? Even questioning at times if God cared about me at all. Was God even real? Because, if so, how could this God that everyone said was so amazing and wonderful allow a child to go through what I was experiencing? Eventually, falling into the downward spiral of lower and lower self-esteem, living in a home I did not have a choice in choosing, led me to become truant most of my junior high school days. This behavior eventually landed me placed on probation and in and out of the juvenile detention center, a girls' group home and then foster care for a second time. I would stay away from my mother's house anywhere I could stay, and she would report me as a runaway to my probation officer. When I would go to juvenile court, there was never a goal of rehabilitation, she was not present as a supporter for me, she just wanted me sent away to wherever was recommended by probation and agreed with the judge so that she would not have to deal with me. We had a very tumultuous relationship and I never felt supported or treated as if I was a daughter. It was as if we were strangers to each other.

As I grew into a young teenager, I found myself always comparing myself with those around me and I felt there was just no purpose in competing. Feelings of being unworthy are what primarily caused me to skip school. I thought I was the ugliest girl in the world, that I had no talent to pursue or that anything worthwhile stood out about me. *My own mother does not care for me so why would anyone else?*

I would compare myself to the girls at school, on the streets, even in the music videos, and thought those abilities to make life enjoyable and those "looks" were too distant for me to attain. There was nothing that I found special about myself. Feeling trapped in my own mind with no escape, within myself, I was in a constant battle. The battle of the mind can be the strongest battle, there is no running from that, and I knew there was no winning—I was simply ensnared in a net of negativity.

Chapter 3—Changing Tones . . . But Not Really

At the age of thirteen I met my first boyfriend, whom we will call Carl. When I met Carl, he was eighteen, in college, and working at an electronics store in one of the local shopping centers in town. I was taken aback that someone so attractive in my eyes was attracted to me and was showing me his attention. It made me feel—even if just for a second— that maybe I was not so unattractive and maybe my awkward personality was not so awkward. A girl name Cierra that I met at school, would accompany me to see him after school. The way Carl's eyes would sparkle like bright stars in the night at me as I walked thru the door, made me feel as If I was above the clouds in the air like the stars.

Carl complemented me, wanted me, and I felt I had won the jackpot. Although I did not see what Carl saw, it did not matter. I had someone interested in me and giving me love and affection, giving his time, and it seemed that was what was so long overdue and what I needed most at that point in my life. If Carl had asked me to walk to the moon and back, I just would have asked, "When do you want me to leave?" We all think our first love, or what we interpret as love at the time, is the be all end all for us. Nothing else could compare, because at the time that is all we know. As time went on, I would soon come to know that this relationship with Carl was not as monogamous as what I had led myself to believe. He was everything for me, but it was not the same for him. The thought was not there that a young man just starting out in his life, attending college with the curiosity of exploring the world, would be serious about a committed relationship. I lost my virginity to Carl because at that time he was giving me an alternative outlet to my reality.

There was no pressure from him; it was something I wanted to do. However, I also felt that was something I needed to do as well, in order to solidify our relationship. Otherwise, I felt I might possibly risk losing him. Eventually I found him out, even caught him in the act of entertaining other ladies. Carl lived in a fraternity house and one night I snuck out to unexpectedly surprise him. The door to his dorm room did not have a peak hole and when he opened the door and realized it was me, he quickly shut it in my face. I began banging the door with my fists and kicking the door with my feet screaming as other residents of the fraternity came out their rooms and into the hallway, alarmed by the kerfuffle. My body temperature hot on a winter night and forehead dripping of sweat from the workout of beating his door, I shouted, "What girl do you have in there?!" He eventually came out of his room and we went into the stone stairwell at the end of the hallway to talk, where a cold but needed breeze hit my warm face. I expressed my love for him, still crying inconsolably. I was not in a place where I loved and respected myself, and I was angry. I was not even sure if it mattered a lot to me or did not matter what he chose to do outside of us. All I knew was that I wanted to keep this man in my life. There was no one for me to confide in, to talk to or get advice from. So, to me, wanting the intimacy of confiding him was normal. I allowed this charade to go on until I was fifteen years old, and the relationship was forcefully terminated because I was sent to a girl's group home in a northern town three hours away from the Twin Cities of Minnesota in which I was ordered by the judge to reside for six months for a probation violation.

I did not see it then but that was God's way of bringing me out that relationship. While I was with Carl, I never stopped to look or think if there was something better for me. I seemed to have tunnel vision; all I could see was what was in front of me and I was not wise enough— like other fifteen-year-olds to look any further ahead. Let alone within. In fact, I am sure I did not really want to do either because I was too frightened of what I might find. I did not expect good things to happen for me because so far, they never had. When I was placed in a position to separate from Carl so unexpectedly, I felt as though I was losing my mind. I could not eat, I could not think about anything but him and what he was doing, and what he would be doing with me far away. I knew my world would not be the same and that I had to lose the only person I loved that I felt loved me back. Or so I thought.

I had my fifteenth birthday while assigned to the group home but spent it in the mental health ward of the hospital, because just weeks after being placed, I tried to run away by jumping out of a second-floor window, confident the December snow appeared to be ample enough to cushion my fall. It did not and I broke my leg. The jump I took required surgery, placing a metal rod, with pins and screws in my ankle in order for my leg to heal properly with the damage I caused. I was in a cast for three and a half months, in physical therapy for a month, and walking with a limp, relearning how to run. Six months later I completed the program at the group home and was back at the house with my mother who was not welcoming me back with open arms and made it clear she did not want me in her home. I was a minor so that forced her into the position where she didn't have a choice. She always was sure to remind me she could not wait for me to be eighteen so that I could get out of her house. She also dropped constant reminders that her life was not what it should have been because she chose to have children. I remember her telling me one day as she sat in the darkness of the kitchen, "I would have my master's degree by now, had I not had children." My reply to that was "We did not ask you to have us. I can see after one, maybe two kids you might decide having children is not for you, but then you went on to have five kids and that is not our fault."

When my probation officer took me back to her house, it was an issue to my mother for me to bring in my few belongings and possessions that I had accumulated while I was sent away. For an hour, my probation officer and I stood outside the screen door as my mother guarded the entry, pointing to my belongings on the ground as if they were a pile of trash, repeating that my things were not allowed in her house. She was always just so evil without any potentially valid reason. It was already bad enough that she had discarded into the trash the few things that meant anything to me when I was sent away. I am sure my mother was hoping I would never return.

During my residency at the group home, we were required on Sundays to write two letters to send home. I would send letters to my mother apologizing and telling her what was happening in the program. I sent cards I had made and dollars I had earned from doing my chores for my two little sisters, and my little brother, whom she had when she remarried. For seven months, I was the only resident who never received any letters in return. Neither did I have any phone calls from home, and my calls and voicemails would go unanswered. There were no visits from loved ones either. When I completed my program in the girls group home, I was happy to leave, but then again, what did I have to look forward to? Carl was no longer around, and I was back with my mother, this woman who carried me for nine months and gave birth to me but only showed me resentment, regret, and hatred to no end. There was a claim that she had been raped when I was conceived but there was never a confirmation to me of that story. My mother always made me feel as if I was the worst person that ever walked the face of the earth, that even if I was doing well, that was not good enough because I needed to do better. There was no winning either way. I would often wonder about my biological father and his family and if I had known them would I be embraced with open arms and some form of the truth of why he was not in my life.

I was feeling hopeless and pretty much stuck in the same cycles all over again. There was no self-reflection into what I would want for myself going forward. It was difficult for me to see past the pain in my heart. I felt lonely, and I did not want to feel what I felt. I just wanted to move around so that I could not feel anything and escape the only reality of my being I had known. The only thing that changed a bit within this time was my self-confidence. That change, however, was not authentic. It was based on the fact since Carl had given me attention, that was something I could have again. So I started attempting to keep myself up with my outside appearance, not so much for myself, but to attract the attention I was so desperately seeking. I was trying to fill an empty space by feeling wanted by men. I was like a walking broken mirror. There were many pieces of me that were not intact, some broken, barely hanging on, yet still visible.

I received what I was looking for, but not in a productive way because what I got was not good for me. What I ran into did not feed my soul, help me to become a better person for myself or motivate me to do anything differently. It was more like a path of regression with different characters. I did not care because it was the attention for me, the being noticed, accepted in some form, feeling like I was good at something—even it was just getting a man's attention—that counted. Does this sound familiar to you? Seeking love and affection no matter the cost? Not realizing you are on a downhill spiral, setting yourself up for more heartbreak and turmoil? I found myself in all types of different entanglements because of the love I did not have in my home circumstances. It is difficult to know what healthy love feels like when you have yet to experience it or have never had a positive example of it. Even if what someone is saying to you is true, when you have no knowledge or sense of discernment within yourself, how can you realize or recognize whether it is truthful or not.

CHAPTER 4—
DIFFERENT REFLECTIONS IN THE MIRROR

Hang on for the Ride.

Now that I have given you a glance into the background of my early years, and an idea of the foundation of my emotional and mental molding, I want to take you on a journey through some of the types of relationships and situations that are possible for you to land in when you do not have a clear identity or solid foundation of your true self. When you do not stand for something, you will fall for anything. When there is not a target, you can only shoot aimlessly. This may or may not reflect your current or previous situation, but I am confident in this next chapter we will surely give you a stepping stone, if not a ladder, of how to step over and avoid obstacles as well as avoid wasting time which we can never get back. I found myself in some relationships and quagmires I never would have believed I could actually find myself in. I would have thought *that could never be me.* Unfortunately, however, I did not avoid a lot of heartache, I missed healing opportunities, took the wrong turns and suffered a good deal of pain. I wasted time that should have been spent fixing what was broken inside me and getting to truly know myself as a unique person. But above all, I wasted time when I could have been building an intimate relationship with God.

CHAPTER 5—DICEY SITUATIONS

I know you may hate to hear it Sis, but we must take it for the team sometimes. We may not be able to quickly pinpoint that funny feeling in our heart and the churning in our gut, but ultimately it all starts with you. Whether you call yourself a young lady, or a woman, what's most important is our individuality, and how we truly view ourselves. So you find yourself in a particular situation that is not going anywhere, life is feeling stagnant, and you can feel the person you are, not the one you want to be. You can dream that there must be something better for you, yet you continue to hold onto the hope that the sparks you imagine will surface and that something will magically change whether it comes from within you or the situation. More times than not, it is both.

I believe we, as women, have our slight ideas of how this wild man of a beast may be right for us. He's sweet and charming when he wants to be, but other times you just cannot stand him. You love him and hate him, at the same time. The version of the role a man should play in our lives can come from our fathers, male family members, what society shows us, or even what we play into with our own imagination. This brings us to our first type of relationship we can have when involved with a man, The Smasher. This is the type of guy who just wants to have sexual relations, is pretty much straight to the point about it and offers nothing else. Do not be fooled as this type of man does not always come across as a total jerk, because he can be gentlemen-like. However, do not expect to be wined and dined either. More times than not, you will get his phone calls later in the evening when the affairs that matter most to him are taken care of, and it is time to settle the day down. Because he may not be completely distasteful, you feel there is some type of connection, in most situations, drawn from the sexual and physical chemistry between you. You may have extended an offer to make lunch plans or perhaps attend an event together, but his idea of a plan with you is Netflix and chill, which will still lead him into what he primarily wants from you. Sex. He may be in a position where he wants to settle down, just not with you. There is no intention to pursue anything else to deepen the relationship. It is just what it is—a nice guy's booty call. Generally, this type of guy will not want to be seen with you out in the public or introduce you to his family and friends because he knows that this is not a long-time investment. He knows he will not be around for the long haul. *He's there for a good time, not a long time.*

In this same smasher group, you also have the straight shooter and there is no finessing the situation. Inside a relationship such as this, there is not any genuine effort to get to know you as a person and there's not much intimate talk or questions about what is going on with you in your particular personal life. If, at any point, you need any kind of help, like a magician's trick, he will disappear in the snap of a finger. Or he may just distance himself for a few days while you try to figure out your situation only to find him return as if nothing ever happened. When you present him with a problem you are dealing with, there is an unspoken vibe of "that's tough." He is not offering any type of solution or input or as much as an encouraging word because realistically he does not care. You can also see this type of relationship as some will configure it: "friends with benefits." On your part, this type of commitment can scream low self-esteem, without values or boundaries. It is committing to a free for all.

Why do men indulge in this and purposely seek out these types of "situationships" with women? Because it leaves them with an "available" woman and a good time without any real accountability, commitment, or responsibility. Are you having a "wow" moment right now? Do not be afraid ladies; this ride is just getting started and we have not even touched the surface. If you find yourself in this situation as you read, you need to end it now because I can tell you that it will only lead you to a broken heart, confusion, and unmet expectations. The lines get blurry fast with this type of "arrangement," because of the physical and sexual connection. You are more than this, Queen. Do not put a $3.00 price tag on your priceless self.

Next to the Smasher is —and as bad as it gets— in terms of unmet expectations and not respecting yourself for the Queen that you are— is The Married Man. This is on top for one of the worst relationships in which to get yourself muddled. Again, this screams low-self-esteem, even if you feel you are secure in yourself. Most likely, you honestly know that you are not getting a whole man, but a piece of him and you are, in all reality, sharing him with another woman. So he is just not yours. Personally, I enjoy eating a good steak, but I do not want it if I can only have a corner edge of it. I would rather you not allow me to have the steak at all. Do you not deserve a man of your own who will hold you in the highest regard? It is disrespectful to yourself and to his wife, there are no boundaries, and you are extending yourself at someone else's convenience, as well as setting yourself up for trauma and trust issues. The married man with a woman on-the-side relationship fulfills the true definition of his having his cake and eating it too. Again, in some cases, you have your straight shooters. They will tell you upfront that I am a married man, and I am looking for an extramarital affair that is simply sexually based. More times than not

however that is not the way the case is laid out and presented. These men come as predators seeking a thrill. They will prey on women who lack confidence, are unsure of themselves, emotionally unstable, and often come from unstable homes and backgrounds themselves.

Women can be gullible and too immature to see the man for who he is. The married man puts on a facade that he himself is broken and unhappy in his marriage. He will often say his wife doesn't understand him and hint that he wants a divorce. Yet he stays in the marriage to maintain the financial security and status that the marriage presents to others with an image of himself with the wife in tow. These husbands have no intentions of leaving their wives, especially when there are children involved, because it is never a cut and dry situation. In dealing the cards of his manipulative moves, the husband will portray himself as the victim and that he is stuck in a situation from which he cannot extract himself.

The reality is that the husband desires to have a sexual partner on the side for his own selfish pleasure, perhaps hoping to fulfill what he may feel he is lacking in his marriage. It does us well to remember that this dishonest husband stood at an altar and took vows before God to be true to his bride. These types of men are masters manipulators. It takes an extremely disloyal, dishonest man to carry on an extra-marital affair and then go home to his wife like nothing has happened. In some audacious cases, he may even bring the other woman into the home that he shares with his wife and family.

Deceiving someone and cheating is wrong on all levels, but this relationship holds a higher regard because God holds marriage to a high standard. Hebrews 13:4 says, (AMPC version) "Let marriage be held in honor (esteemed worthy, precious, of great price, and especially dear) in all things. And thus let the marriage bed be undefiled (kept dishonored)."

Digging into this type of relationship can be an extremely sensitive subject. Like politics. You may have been or are on the opposite side of infidelity, and instead be the woman who knows your husband is stepping outside the marriage to engage in affairs with other women. I am in no way, shape, or form, dismissing the responsibility of the women who participates in adultery. This is simply a warning, a reflection of a type of relationship that we, as single women, can find ourselves in when we do not hold high standards within ourselves. Infidelity has caused a lot of broken trust for many women as well as broken homes for children, and no matter what side of the fence you find yourself on—the participating deceitful cheat or the one deceived by a cheater, it is wrong. There is no way around it, no matter how well the wolf in sheep's clothing is disguised. You deserve better Queen, so muster up the strength to get out because you are better than that. That is called "settling" and you do not have to. To the woman hurting behind these doors, children involved or not, you can exit stage left. Romans 8:37 (AMPC version) says, "Yet amid all these things we are more than conquerors and gain surpassing victory through Him Who loved us." Do not let the fear of "Can I continue life without my husband?" Or "Will my children be able to withstand such a transition," be a determining factor in your decision because with God, you are more than a conqueror and He will take care of you. No doubt about it.

In the type of games that go on when you decide to become the "other woman," you will often misconstrue the situation, thinking the adulterer, whom you are seeing, is perfect, and the wife is the problem. It is easy to fall into the arms of a man who is flattering you with his attention. You may tell yourself, "It's ok— and is not cheating because he is such a 'good guy,'" and he just wants to be happy." That is just an excuse to turn a blind eye. Even more so, these situations will have you trying to live up to his expectations at any and every regard to try to fill the void he says he is feeling so that you can be his heroine.

And how you get him may be how you will lose him. What makes you exempt from becoming the one cheated upon. If he cheated with you, he may cheat on you as well, with yet another woman. Is he trustworthy after all? There is a problem within himself that feels unfulfilled and that needs personal addressing. There is not anything that you or any other woman can do for him that will fill that void. It can put you in a frame of mind where you feel committed to the uncommitted and you would not dare speak to another man or carry on another relationship outside of the one with the married man because you are putting all your eggs into this basket that is already full and technically unavailable. Where do you fit in? Would you want your husband carrying on such an affair? Would you want your daughter to stay with someone who is not being faithful to her? Place yourself on the other end of the spectrum and think about how would you feel if you found out your husband was not being true to his marriage vows and was having an outside relationship, that in some cases could result in sexually transmitted diseases and even pregnancies and children outside the marriage? Why do you, as a woman, find that this type of behavior is okay to accept? Why? Because we ourselves are broken and seeking validation of some form. Feeling as if you are the prize and that he truly does not want his wife leads to a false sense of high esteem. I know this from experience. We may come from broken homes ourselves, so the feeling of empathy and sympathy is not there to feel responsible for another broken home. There are unmet dreams in our own realities, and jagged perceptions of our true selves as worthy individuals. We are hurt, stuck in our own unresolved trauma from the times we were not rescued when we were hurting. Therefore, it is not a concern for someone else to be hurting.

Yes, there are also times when a woman is not given a choice to know outright and is blindly led by a man she has interest in who has presented and perceived himself as a single man when in truth he is not. Are you breaking it off when that truth comes to the surface? Or are you now becoming a willing participant? There are some married men who will "pay to play" and others who will make it clear you are not getting a thing honey, but you can call me when your expectations have changed. Then there is the married one who will do little things like buy you a designer handbag or Chanel perfume and treat you as special just enough to keep you quiet for a while off his back, distracting you from the real problem and keeping you at bay. Is that worth your soul? Is that worth being delayed, even excluded from the man that God has for you because you are playing around with someone else's husband? Are you only worth the value of a handbag and a bottle of perfume? Is it worth it to only have half a man for half an evening before he takes off like a thief in the night? It is easy to go with the flow until the shoe is on another's foot. It has not been my proudest moment but I have been involved with a married men, so I come sharing from personal experience. It is a low moment when after you have hooked up with a man that is not yours, to see him checking the time as he hurries and scrambles to find his clothing that has been scattered across the floor or he drives faster than normal to drop you off from dinner so that he can make it back home in time and will not raise suspicion. Or what if he is faced with a problem such as your car breaking down and you find your call to him goes unanswered because he is at home with his family. I am here to tell you Queen, you are worth so much more. So, repent wholeheartedly before the Lord and let him go.

Everyone has their vision and version of what success looks like. Imagine you are sitting in a painting class. The instructor has one image that the whole class will focus on painting. Everyone is not going to use the same sketching technique or brushstroke to reproduce the image on display. We all have our own walks and journeys which is normal in life and completely fine, but it is your duty to distinguish what the blueprint of your plan looks like to get what you are desiring. God has the final say in the development, but you can't expect tweaks and changes until after you begin to put in the effort to build. After the married man relationship, I want to change tone just a bit, which leads us into exploring, "The Helper."

When I was 18, I became a mother from a situation that I cannot even call a relationship with a married man named Jack, who was thirty years my senior. As I just explained the typical relationship with a married man that you can find yourself in when you do not set self-esteem, boundaries and expectations of yourself to a high level, mine was literally a "fly by night" situation. Jack would pick me up and the ultimate purpose was to have sexual relations. One time he picked me up and I was not in the mood to be sexual with him and expressed this to him as we sat in his car. Sitting in the driver's seat he rubbed my shoulders and he told me, "There is no reason to come if we do not have sex because I am taking a big risk to get away from home to come and see you." We had never been out to eat together or anywhere in a normal casual setting to hang out, but he would buy me little gifts to keep me at bay or put me in a motel for a night when my mother and I would fight, of course spending "time with me," before leaving me alone to go home to his family.

After several encounters I found myself pregnant at 17. I began to feel taken advantage of because he was so much older than me, and I ended the "relationship" with him. I found out a week later I was pregnant. I was caught off guard with the news when I went to the clinic, in fact I was not sure what I was expecting with a missed period. I had asked the nurse for another test. At my urging I was given another pregnancy test and by the third request the nurse told me, "No matter how many tests you take that will not change the results." I sat on the edge of the exam table bed and cried, wailing, my body limp to where someone could blow on me and I would fall over. Having a baby in this way was not my ideal thought of how I would one day have a child, but the baby was coming, and I was left alone with the biological father of my child refusing to be involved. I had what we call a "Deadbeat Dad." He even denied he was the father of my baby. He was not willing to be there physically for either my son or I and contributed nothing willingly in terms of finances.

The wife of this man requested that I have an abortion at her expense. I was raised to believe that abortion was immoral and incorrect. Today I consider myself pro-choice, only because it is not my position to be the judge to determine another's decision in this regard, but despite what I was raised to believe, I wanted to have my baby because I wanted someone to love and someone who would love me back. I was legally homeless and in high school taking a two-hour bus ride each way every day to complete my diploma.

At that point, I had been in a few "situationships" that led nowhere, and I was still not looking at the picture that mattered most. Myself. Now I felt I was faced with not having time for those thoughts even if I wanted to indulge them because I had a child coming who I now needed to figure out how to provide for—as well as find a stable home for—and become a mother to—my child!

Although I never had a relationship with my own mother by the grace of God, mothering instincts came natural to me. I was more scared of facing myself then I was of becoming a mother. I questioned if I was even deserving of this beautiful blessing because of the situation in which he was created. I did not have anyone or anything and I knew that he deserved better than what I could offer.

While I was pregnant with my son, after my mom put me out, I stayed with an aunt named Linda, my mother's sister. She did not welcome me in her home but was tolerant of me, walking around me in similar and eerie silence just like my mother had always done, ignoring the fact I existed except with a stone face of disgust and annoyance. I was uncomfortable and stressed being at her house, so I stayed at two different shelters after leaving her.

The first shelter was a place to be able to sleep at night and during the day, residents needed to figure it out until 9pm that evening. It was not clean, and I slept on the edge of the bed frame, scared to use the blankets and covers provided to wrap myself in, so I slept in my clothes with a sweater, my jacket as my pillow and was cold most nights as I cried myself to sleep feeling hopeless. I also shared a room with four other individuals. The second shelter I stayed in was for homeless teens. I shared a room with another girl, but I felt safe, it was clean, the staff was compassionate and helpful. However, once I delivered my son, I could no longer stay as the program was not formed for families. In my third trimester I stopped going to my prenatal appointments. I look back and think a part of me felt the baby would come when he was ready, giving me more time to figure out where we both could live. After I passed 41 weeks, with no symptoms of labor in the forecast, I made a doctor appointment and was admitted to the hospital the same day due to low amniotic fluid. My labor was induced; however, I was not dilating at the speed the doctor was expecting to see. Suddenly doctors and nurses came rushing into my room urgently requesting I sign which seemed like never ending forms, and I was wheeled upstairs for an emergency cesarean birth. My son's heart rate was dropping, and he was delivered within ten to fifteen minutes later.

Holding Michael in my arms for the first time I had mixed emotions of happiness and fright. My support system in the delivery room was a woman name Carmen, who was a doula and someone that I met with a few times in the earlier stages of pregnancy. This birth, a moment in life that was so special I essentially shared with a stranger. After the birth, I never saw Carmen again.

Michael and I stayed in the hospital for over a week, due to my cesarean birth and Michael being placed in the NICU- newborn intensive care unit because of his lack of eating and low birth weight. I was not in a hurry to leave the hospital because I was not sure where we would go, as we did not have a place to call "home."

If there was ever a time it was necessary to place my pride to the side, this was it. I Realized I needed to go back to Linda's house because I did not want my newborn to be in a shelter. I could only tolerate being unwanted for two weeks after going back to her house.

I remember the day I left, I rode the city bus with Michael sound asleep in his stroller, fed and changed with no worries. I cried as I rode the bus starting from when the sun beamed in the mid-afternoon, until the moon and stars sprinkled the sky. Back and forth on the route for hours because I did not know what to do or where we could go. It was not that I didn't put any effort during my pregnancy to secure permanent housing, but the income-based housing locations I signed up for had waiting lists. I couldn't work full time because I was finishing school, and now I had a baby for whom I did not have childcare, in order to be able to work full time. With no other choices, I went to my old neighborhood where I lived with my mom. She had sold the house and moved to Rhode Island with my younger siblings immediately after she no longer had to me to deal with, just as she had said she would do. I reached out to Darla, the mother of two girls that I was previously friends with and shared moments with when I stayed with my mom. Darla welcomed me with open arms no questions asked, opinions or comments released. She offered her basement to Michael and me, which was finished and furnished and had a private bathroom. I thought I would be happy once I settled somewhere safe and welcoming. I could at least be at ease to think what my potential next plans were, but instead I was looking into the face of deep depression. All I could manage to do was change Michael's diaper and fix bottles for him. How I mustered up that strength only by the grace of God. I would lie in bed with the lights off, besides a clock, I could not distinguish night from day. I would not come out of the basement to feed myself. It was comfortable for me to stay in bed all day because I did not have to face reality or think about anything.

After a week Darla came down the basement and turned all the lights on and sat on the edge of the bed. She was a heavier set woman who always wore scrubs because she worked as a registered nurse and had shoulder length thick black hair which she usually wore with two cornrows braided to the back. She said to me, "I understand you are going through a lot and you are depressed but sleeping all day with this baby is not good for either of you. I want you to get in a habit of getting up every day and do at least one thing that will help both of you move forward and get engaged with your son. I don't mind you staying in my home but sleeping every day is not going to help change anything."

I said in a soft whisper, "It's so hard." I cry right in this moment as I write this and remember. My mother had once gone to her home and tried to bad mouth me as a terrible person, I assume in an attempt to get her daughters to stop being my friend. Darla was gentle, genuine, supportive, kind, soft spoken, understanding. She held me like a baby as I wept in her arms, while I held Michael sleeping peacefully in mine. I will always be forever grateful for her. It was that conversation that gave me the motivation to get up every day and do something to help move myself forward. A month later I was accepted into a transitional housing program for women who were single or had no more than one child up to the age of five. I think this point was the first time I sighed a breath of relief.

When my son was three months old, I met someone whom we will call "Mark." When I met Mark, I was downtown getting on the city bus, and he helped me by lifting my son who was in his stroller onto the bus. I had an hour-long bus ride to the other side of town, and I engaged in a conversation with Mark that I felt I wanted to continue, so by the time I was getting off the bus, we were exchanging numbers. Since the conception of Michael and all the confusion that came along with that situation, with Jack, the man whom I now called the "sperm donor," I was focused on gaining some type of stability for our basic needs. Having a man around for the first time was on the bottom of the list, but it was surprisingly refreshing to have Mark notice me just three months after having a baby. My first thought was he knew I had a child, so let us see where this could go, and he seemed pleasant enough. There was no courting of the relationship and we just fell into spending time with each other each day. Mark did not have a car or a job and with my son and his needs growing, I knew I needed to get a job because welfare was only getting us so far. Although the transitional housing program was a place to live, it was limited for long term housing needs. Mark was willing to help watch my son while I worked a retail job at the mall. He was okay with cooking, cleaning, helping to change diapers and feeding, but he did nothing towards becoming a provider and played video games all day. I never stopped to think what my expectations would be for myself and my child to have a man become one with us. It is critical to set boundaries and expectations for any new person in your life when you have children involved. It is not just about you anymore. I knew what I was feeling was not right. I knew that I did not want to be taking care of a grown man as the only breadwinner, no matter how much he "helped" household-wise. We never lived together, but I was allowed to have company at the transitional housing facility or Michael and I would go over to where a friend allowed Mark to stay in an extra bedroom.

Remember we talked about that churning feeling of the gut? I felt so unsettled with this arrangement, although I still was not sure what life would look like for me going forward, I knew this was something I did not want long term. Subsequently, the relationship turned very toxic because of my unmet expectations, constant frustration and his stance on not trying to be or do better. I lost respect for him as a man. Once again, I found myself in a situation I did not want to be in, but the desire for attention and affection and to have another adult around me clouded my judgement.

We live in a society today where it is now normal for gender roles to be reversed, which is ok, but you need to decide what is best for you. The playing field should still level out and that was not the case with Mark. God once again brought me out of a position I had no business being in when one day Mark and I had a big fight, and he went back to where his family lived out of state. We never spoke or saw each other again.

Although he was not what I wanted, I had become so dependent on that relationship, it amounted to another heartbreak all over again. I felt the pain that I had not felt since Carl. Still at this point in my life, I was not overly confident in myself as a person. I was still struggling with the hurt from my family, both extended and intermediate, specifically the rejection of love from my own mother, and the resentment I felt having to raise a child on my own. There were all these *underlined, unaddressed, unresolved* issues so where was the possibility for me to know what I should be looking for and how it should feel, let alone what it would look like if I came across it? I was still driving with my eyes closed. Instead of channeling that hurt and turning it around for the positive and learning from yet another failed experience, I became rebellious. I figured this was the life that God had set out for me, having it hard, having pain, being let down, not being good enough and being alone was all I ever knew and maybe it was all I deserved. I believed that at some point in life I had messed up badly and it was too late to make things right. Have you ever been at a point in your life, maybe even in this moment as you read, where no matter how much you try, it just seems like things will not shift in your favor? Have you sat and asked God to reveal his plan for you? Have you thought: what are some of the same moves I am making to keep getting into these similar situations with similar roles and characters? Have you looked yourself in the mirror and honestly and wholeheartedly asked yourself, *Who Am I?*

Visualize what life would look like for you going forward? What things are you holding onto in your heart that is impacting the choices you are making and the people you are making them with? I wish I would have stopped and asked myself those questions which I needed to seek answers to at that point in my life, but I did not. Stop yourself in your tracks right now. I am offering you the insight to dive into and honestly ask yourself those questions. It is important to get a clear understanding of who you are and where your life is heading.

Harboring negative feelings of yourself, holding on to what others have done to hurt you, regretting the choices you have made that you wish you could take back, and not welcoming Jesus to come full circle into every part of your life will keep you stagnant. Even in the toughest of times, it is better to sit through the discomfort in the comfort of His grace then to attempt to fight the battle alone. Battles can be graceful too with God on your side. Accept Jesus into your life, draw close to Him and He will draw even closer into you. He knows exactly how you feel and the ins and outs that you yourself cannot even put together. Have you ever stopped to think it is your mild, meek faith that is keeping you from receiving what God wants for you? Maybe you believe that He will come through for you but just enough to barely scratch the surface or that your faith is not even the size of a mustard seed? It is the devil's tactic to use what he can to keep you from allowing God to be the center of your life. The enemy uses your weaknesses, your doubts, fears, troubles, past against you because satan wants to see you in prison and held captive, missing out on the glory for your purposed soul. I know grammatically it is correct to capitalize satan, but we will not give satan any satisfaction, so he will be addressed with a lower-case s in this book. In my case, I allowed the enemy to use my need for love, attention, and the desire to have someone in my life whom I thought would care about me enough to distract my attention from God and the true purpose for my life. We all resist change and it is difficult to change so we keep spinning our wheels in place.

Fear is the devil's playground, and I was fearful for a lot of my years. Fearful of being alone, fearful of not being good enough or pretty enough, fearful of what others thought of me, fearful of the unknown or what the future held, so I held onto what I knew because I could see what I was dealing with, it was familiar, and I was comfortable in the familiar.

Chapter 6—Is this Marriage?

When my ex-husband Sam, and I met, I was twenty years old, Michael was now a two and a half year-old-toddler, and I thought he was the best thing that had happened to my son and me since sliced bread, that finally the chance for a piece of happiness and stability had risen to the occasion.

We met while working at Target; he worked in the bakery as the baker, and I worked in the deli, product production. We started off as co-workers who took our lunch breaks together. I genuinely enjoyed spending time with Sam and one afternoon while we sat and ate our lunch in a McDonald's booth he asked me, "If it is ok, I would love to take you and your son out for dinner sometime." With my eyes batting and cheeks blushing, I accepted his invitation with no hesitation. Later that week I chose for us to have dinner at my favorite Chinese buffet and soaked up the energy he displayed with Michael. I was attempting to think forward, my mind racing like a gerbil on a wheel, and did not want to repeat what I had experienced with Mark. With Sam, I was presented with a man who would be suitable to be a father to Michael. He had a job and his own transportation, and he was initially respectful of all the baggage I came with. He showed genuine interest in being a part of my life, as well as my son's. At this point, I literally was emotionally and mentally drained from all the relationships and encounters that I had previously, and I figured it was best to settle down with this guy who was older than me and had the willingness to settle down with us. I was certain that this was the right choice due to the fact that someone older was better for me and I thought I would bypass a lot of the negativity of the growth process in a man who was closer to my age. Physically, he was not my ideal type. Sam stood 5 feet 5 Inches tall compared to my 5 feet 8 Inches. He was of lighter brown skin and my preference was dark brown skin men. He also had dreads that fell past his waist, and I was normally drawn to men with low fade haircuts or bald fades. However attraction grew, and I was able to look past physical qualities that were not on my list, because of his character and his willingness to help me with my child, and especially because he immediately took to my son as if he was his own blood.

By this time my job at Target allowed me to move out of transitional housing into my first market rate rent one-bedroom apartment that had an indoor pool. Sam who moved from Washington to Minnesota to help with his grandchildren, lived with his eldest son and his wife as they could not afford daycare and with three children, a two-income home was dire. After a series of visits, bringing his clothes over to stay one night, accompanied by another invitation to stay the night and bringing more clothes, I eventually invited Sam to stay with me, which I signified as a step of being officially in a relationship. Immediately, upon Sam moving out, his son and his wife began throwing boulders at us, not stones, mostly over our age difference. Sam was twenty-eight years my senior. Also, due to the fact his relationship status had changed and now we were as one unit, he was not readily available to watch the grandkids whenever they wanted nor to help financially as he no longer lived in their home. The tension between Sam's son and daughter-in-law and me moved to social media which was MySpace during that time. You would have thought someone was messing with someone's man or woman rather than a "family dispute." To this day I am not sure where the anger stemmed from, although I have a few inclinations, but I know for sure it wraps around not letting the past be the past and not dealing with unresolved personal trauma, specifically from childhood. It's like painting a picture of a life that is not as colorful as it is painted. Like with my mom, the behavior has more to do with someone's own internal struggles than with the person who is on the receiving end of another's unresolved struggles and traumas.

People always talk about red flags. But looking for red flags was not even a part of my thought process in my twenties. It was in me to be a hard fighter for love because I craved it so deeply. My position was that the more stones that were thrown meant the harder I should try no matter what the situation was. Again, just driving with eyes closed. As time went on, before I knew it, things were happening that I never thought would become factors in this "happily-ever-after" I'd envisioned. But I was determined to "ride it out" with this man because we had similar issues of abandonment, as he was adopted as a baby.

Sam grew up confused about why his biological mother did not want him but kept other children she had. He was confused over his ethnicity position being biracial. His hair was too fine to be seen as black and then he was considered "too black"— having been raised with African American parents—to be considered Japanese. I believe that is how we bonded due to our positions in childhood, plus I could prove to his family that I was not going anywhere. A year and a half into our relationship, I became pregnant with our first child together, Mason, and a breath of fresh air clung to me carrying this new life. Having Mason's father on board was inviting because at that time I was going through a life altering situation where Michael was temporarily taken away from me and put into foster care. History attempting to repeat itself, in a form of a "generational curse." I was dealing with a lot of frustration battling Sam's family, dealing with our relationship, working full-time, the sperm donor bringing me to court to get child support reduced although he was not an active "father," and the daycare center was calling me at work for every little thing my son was doing from throwing tantrums to wetting himself.

At that time the "sperm donor" was listed as an emergency contact and when the daycare would contact the sperm donor, he'd refuse to leave work. Still at this point, he was pretty much nonexistent in my son's life. Another phone call one day pushed me into an unfortunate incident. When I came to pick my three-year-old son up, I spanked him at the daycare and the staff called the police on me. It was inside the daycare with several witnesses, but there were also lies told that I took my son to the parking lot and threw him into the car and punched him which was not at all true. Nonetheless, I was charged with malicious punishment of a child and my son was taken to foster care for three months.

During that time I was given two years of probation, 100 hours of community service—which was hard for me to do so my probation was violated—and I did two weeks in the work house. I was ordered to complete parenting class and to work with our case manager on getting Michael evaluated for any special needs because at the time his speech was delayed. At that same time as the child protection case, our housing stability was at stake because where I rented my first apartment, after moving from another transitional housing program, the management would not renew my lease due to a few late rent payments. As Sam and I were attempting to find a place to live together, we were faced with dealing with his bad credit and lack of rental history and my lack of credit and a gross misdemeanor on my record, making it difficult for us to rent.

From the beginning we were always facing financial issues, setbacks, and consistently falling behind on bills. After losing a few hundred dollars in application fees for being denied apartments, I decided to look on Craigslist for private owners in hopes they would be more understanding of our situation, and not base renting to us off a corporate criteria sheet. We eventually found a duplex to move into and just weeks after being there the electricity was shut off. I got up one morning and flipped the light switch in our bedroom and no light came on as I stood thinking it was a blown bulb. I walked into the kitchen to flip the switch; nothing. I could see lights beaming from the neighbors' windows, so I assumed the fuse had somehow blown in our unit. I walked down to the basement to check the fuse box and as I am coming from the basement I am thinking, " I know the lights were not cut off." I called the gas/electric company and indeed we were disconnected for a $300 past due bill. We did not have the money to pay for the bill until the end of the week, which meant that rent would be late. For the next few days we would use the daylight, then at night we would run an extension cord from the basement to our unit for light, then we'd get up early to disconnect it before the neighbors would get up as they were the in-laws of the owner's wife we were renting from. Sam had his own personal financial burdens and was in extreme debt with the IRS. For a period of time his check was getting garnished. No matter what his check should have been, he was only taking home $300 every two weeks until he caught up with filing his taxes and established an acceptable payment plan to the IRS. I was in between minimum wage jobs that cost more in gas to get to my work than what my check was worth. His family was beyond disrespectful to both of us and there was no respect for our union. It was continuously noted that my son was not a part of the "family name," even if my son was being raised and cared for by a man who was now considered his father. I was ridiculed for having my son temporarily taken away. It was said on a phone call battling back and forth with Sam's daughter-in-law, "you're not a good mom, child protection has proven that." It was hard to have a relationship with Sam when I was fighting to prove we had one, and he was very passive aggressive with the attacks we were facing from his family. Sam took to my son as his own son despite whatever personal vendettas his family felt towards him and his failures in the past. I was on the receiving end of the backlash for who he was not and what he did not do before me, with the two children he had from another relationship, who were grown with families of their own at that point. All of this took a toll on building a solid family unit in our relationship together. I felt that I was going to the battle ground alone when I supposedly had a partner.

If you have experienced something like this or are going through a similar situation and no one has delivered the message, I am here to deliver it. It is not in your place to battle the negativity of your partner's family or those of your own family when you are in relationship with another person, especially once married. When you become one with someone, it does become the two of you against the world, two hearts that beat as one heartbeat. When the union is mutual between the couple, and serious conditions are not present such as drug abuse, any type of violence, whether it is physical, mental, or emotional, and your union is not accepted or respected— it is okay to exclude those individuals from your life. Whether it be adult children, mothers, fathers, grandparents, grandchildren— whomever! I hung onto the hope with Sam that the situation would get better. I tried to get him to see, blood ties or not, that his family was a contributing factor to the strife between us. It came to the point where I had to give an ultimatum. When you are in a relationship, you should never be placed in a situation where you feel that ultimatums need to be made to change a certain circumstance. Both you and your partner should want others around you to help celebrate you, strengthen your union, and encourage you. I thought giving Sam the ultimatum to choose either us or them would help us to regain our footing, but conditions were going to get worse before they became any better.

Our first son together, Mason at the age of five became ill, it seemed, overnight. Thinking it was just a sudden virus or flu, I did not want to take him to the doctor because I did not want to be faced with another bill that I knew we could not afford. We had added another child, Martin and now had three children and were renting a single-family home where we could barely afford to pay the $1200.00 rent, not to mention the need for utilities, food, transportation, and other personal necessities.

After an emergency room visit on Halloween of 2014, Mason would be diagnosed with Type 1 diabetes. I remember when his father called me and told me he was taking our son to the hospital. Our child was barely able to keep his eyes open during the drive, his little body, almost limp. At the time I was working a part time job at Papa Murphy's. I was torn between leaving work and going to the hospital because we could not afford for me to leave early. At the same time, I had enrolled in a two-year program at the local community college for an AAS degree in Medical Administration. However, I was totally ignorant about the disease of diabetes. I had always assumed it was a medical condition that only older people had to deal with, and I was unaware that diabetes was an immune disorder.

I think back how the night before Mason was diagnosed, I remember him literally crawling up the stairs. He had lost so much weight very quickly, and his skin had begun to darken, his eyes bulging, and his face looking sunken. I had no idea that my son was literally dying in front of my face. Mason was placed in the intensive care unit of Children's Hospital, and he was assigned an aide at the hospital to stay by his bedside. As his sugar was brought to a normal level, it was as if my son was a part of an exorcism, as he wasn't in control of his body which was jerking and flailing. I felt helpless at that moment as I stood at the foot of the bed with Sam overlooking. I remember a nurse coming in and asking what our religion was, not knowing that they were anticipating that my baby would not survive this crisis because his blood sugar was over 1400.

At the time I was still engaged in the back-and-forth online beefing with Sam's side of the family and word was passed around about my son and his condition. They mocked his condition in online posts indicating that my evil ways were the reason my son became diabetic, and how grateful they felt to have "healthy" children, although their online beefing was the true evil. Despite what others had to say against me, my son, and his father, by the grace of God and His touch to the doctors and nurses who treated my son, Mason's life was saved, because as the Bible says, "No weapon formed will prosper." The weapon of diabetes formed against Mason, but it did not prosper by him passing away. Glory be to God, Thank you Jesus.

All I could do then was cry, realizing that my baby almost lost his life, and he had a condition that I could not cure, and a completely new way of life lay ahead of us in our role of parenting a diabetic child. Although my relationship with Sam was falling apart and life was not in the greatest place, I would not have chosen anyone else but his father to go through that moment in my life with our son. I was emotionally and mentally distraught from dealing with all that had happened to me with this new diagnosis and during the training for parents of diabetic children, training us how to care for him, I cried most of the time and it was a difficult challenge for several months realizing I was now a mother of a diabetic child and that having insulin, Lantus, syringes, counting carbs, and constant finger poking were now going to be the new norm for my son to deal with. And our role as his parents would be to help navigate and support him. Jesus, that was a very difficult time in my life, but I thank you for carrying me through it.

Sam and I were together for seven years before we wed. There was not a romantic proposal with him on one knee opening a square black box with a diamond. Sam never pressed the issue or determined marriage as a priority when I brought it up. By this time, I was one foot out the door with one foot in, letting the issue die away from me. I think that he felt that as well because now he was in agreement that we should be married. We ended up marrying at a wedding chapel run by two sisters in Florida, just me, him and our boys. I think being in a place that was not our normal home was a distraction from how I felt and kept the problems at bay between us. Being surrounded by beautiful palm trees and a bright sunny warm day helped convince me that maybe this was meant to be. There were dresses available for me to choose from and as I stood in the mirror taking in my reflection with my white dress and long train and veil, looking like a bride, but I did not feel at peace and eager to walk down the aisle. I felt beautiful but in reality, nothing was beautiful about it. At that time my mind-frame wanted to get married because of the children, I felt that getting married would create a Godly intervention and things would get better. I was trying once again to prove to his family that I was not going anywhere, as my mind replayed the taunting from the wife of his son that I would never bear his last name. Later down the line, I would become regretful of all the time I wasted on the back and forth with them because people are going to think and say what they want about you regardless of what is done or isn't done. I put myself through this back-and-forth drama with his family for seven years straight. It did not change anything for me personally or my life. Why do I say "I" put myself through it? Because I made the choice to engage during that time, to snoop on the son's wife page to see what she was saying about me/ us, and I chose to respond to these triggers. Regardless of Sam's passive aggressive actions not to intervene during the span of toxicity. The drama did not gain anything but loss of emotional and mental stability and productive time that should have been spent in many other areas of my life. I was going to war to defend a man who wasn't lifting a finger to fight with me. Can you imagine someone bringing you to the battle ground, with nothing to protect yourself but they just drop you off and leave you there with your enemies? That is how it felt for me. Even in the midst of all the chaos I was having with his family, Sam would buy secret phones to keep in contact with them, the same people who had no respect for him. And he chose to lie to me about where he was going when he would be visiting their house. It truly was a slap to both sides of my face. Even at this point, I still loved him, but it wasn't how I first loved him.

Between trying to work at jobs that were not paying enough and taking care of the kids, we were months behind on rent, enduring a failing relationship, now a failing marriage, and then Sam was terminated from his job. I was dealing with depression and anxiety, now that the van I had was repossessed and my children and I wailed in tears as we found the repo man whisking it away with his tow truck. The relationship I had begun with this man whom I thought was sent as my "Savior" from the life I had known—had now become the worst nightmare for me. No matter how much I tried, how much effort I put in, our relationship could not even be lifted off the ground, let alone into the life I so desperately wanted to build with him. Troubles were once again drowning me and it just seemed as if I could not catch a break.

I was putting forth my best efforts by trying to go to school and trying to figure out a plan for life to be better. I was praying for my marriage to work. I was praying that my husband would put more effort into our marriage and our family, that he would take the progression of the family more seriously. I felt my endless prayers had fallen into some crack between unheard and unanswered. I needed to realize I was in a marriage with someone who did not see nor appreciate my efforts, was not in a true partnership with me, and did not make me feel I was loved, protected, or that we were in this thing called "life" together.

The very fact that someone can constantly hear you cry and not make any effort to do anything differently can be very disturbing. We continued to have the same conversations, but my ideas fell on deaf ears. Everything in me had been drained. The responsibility fell on my shoulders to tend to the children, to be the one to pay the bills and make payment arrangements when needed. The housework for cleaning and washing clothes and dinner rested on me. Sam was oblivious to my need for him to be involved as a helpful hand in raising our family. It made sense for those things to be my job when I wasn't working, but I was working the same forty-hour weeks as he was and his ability to help did not change. I lay in bed by myself night after night, because Sam never came to bed and chose to stay up all night watching TV in the basement. I would cry quietly into my pillow with the lights out and the door shut telling God how miserable I was. I was again in a position where I wanted life to end for me. If God wanted my attention, he surely was now getting my attention undivided.

I have always been spiritual to some extent and have always prayed, but I never sought a deep intimate relationship with God. I never prayed for guidance. I had my mind on what I wanted to happen and prayed that God would do it just the way I had prayed for it, and I was not too open for any suggestions or changes. When challenges would happen in life, it was paralyzing for me and it was hard to pick myself up, time and time again, because I relied solely on my own way of thinking to assure the best outcome. I had to analyze my life and knew that I was tired of being in the same space literally going in circles. Nothing was changing. Nothing much had changed for the better since I met this man. Not for me, not for him and not for us together. I had to ask myself now as the mother of four children, after being with this man for ten years, was this actually the life God wanted me to have? I fought within myself because I knew God hated divorce, and I did not want my children to grow up in a home without both of their parents. I struggled between living up to what I thought God wanted and my feelings of misery within the marriage. Eventually, I came to a crossroads where I had to honestly ask myself was this how I wanted to spend the next ten years? Not even another ten, another year? Another month or even week or day? The answer was a clear *No*, and I was starting to look at a bigger picture for the first time in life instead of just what was before me.

Although I knew that God was not in favor of divorce, I also knew that He did not desire for me to suffer, lost, unfulfilled and unhappy. Looking back, I could see there were so many signs this union was not for me. I lost so much of myself, attempting to make my husband happy that I forgot about my own happiness. Sam almost became my idol because what he wanted is all I wanted to fulfill. He was the center of my world so much so that I could not see myself, just my children and him. I never put myself into the equation. When I would tell him how I felt about where our marriage was and what I felt I was lacking from him as a husband, he would always become defensive instead of being open to change or being open to accept that I was feeling or doing things differently. I constantly heard "go be with those dudes" or in other words go be with someone who has these qualities that you want. Any man who is serious about you, will take your feelings into consideration even if he agrees to disagree. When a man is serious about you, your happiness is important to him as well. He will take action to follow up and be involved after you have expressed your thoughts and feelings as a need for you and the betterment of the relationship. I do not believe it is an unreasonable expectation in a relationship to be wanted and feel wanted not just in the context of sensual words or sexually. Nor is it right to feel that you are in this "supposed" to be committed relationship yet you still feel more alone than if you were not. If you are having repeated conversations about the same issues and concerns but they are not getting addressed or followed up with progress from your partner, you are wasting your time. Eventually those feelings will turn into resentment.

Change does not happen overnight, let alone in the snap of your fingers , but what you should be seeing is a genuine effort and some kind of progress that is not forced or pressured, strides to let you know you have been heard and that it does matter for the relationship to be contained and grow. Actions always speaks louder than words.

I struggled with abandonment and rejection issues because of how my mother had always made me feel in the way she treated me, and with people in general. I just never appeared to fit in anywhere, so when this man who I thought loved me and to whom I thought I mattered, did not fight for me, let alone for our family, it was like another slap to the face. I did not know myself before I entered this relationship, and now I really did not know who I was. I wanted to get back to the person I was before I met him because it was better than who I had become throughout this entire relationship. A lot of times the hardest choices you must make are going to be the best choices you can make. Sometimes you will be so lost in your ways that God will literally have to let everything fall apart in order to pull you off the path to your own self-destruction.

I felt I was in the category I will call; "Doing all the relationship work." The man who will work a job but does not have any ambition to do anything more than that is going to cause you to do all of the real work, the essential work of living with and loving another. That man is emotionally, mentally, and financially immature. He lives in the moment with no thoughts of goals for the future and does not mind living paycheck to paycheck as long there is enough gas to get to work, there is food in the cupboards, and he has a place to call home, despite the lights barely staying on. After the fact I realized the most bothersome issue for me was that he did not pursue or even attempt to develop a closer relationship to God and had no desire for self-improvement. Further down the line I would realize that the marriage was doomed from the beginning because it was a case of two broken people brought together with a co-dependency for each to fill the other's black hole, which inevitably equals a hot mess! In the end, you say what you need to say and if things don't change, then you do what you need to do. Unapologetically. It is one thing to be on two different pages, but when you and the person you are with, or want to be with, are in a different books all together, it is time to start a new chapter on your own.

Chapter 7—Unattached

Now that I felt free and unattached from Sam, I felt my life was renewed and was beginning for me for the first time since the birth of my first child. I completed my program for my Associates Degree in Medical Administration, which was a proud moment for me, the fact that I was able to do it. Between being in a relationship for over ten years and my previous relationships and situations, I would know better by now. Right? The sky is the limit, and I should have been able to soar. I was not afraid of being a single mom to my four boys because I felt groomed to carry the responsibility.

It isn't effective to be in any type of relationship where someone is physically present but is emotionally and mentally unavailable, which is the exact marriage I had found myself in. Besides, I had what I had known previously as "my life" back, with just some added players to my team. Now open only to "friendships," a month after I officially chose to cut ties to my marriage, I met a guy whom we will call Robert. There was again no adjusting to life after a major alteration, I did not take time to reflect on what had occurred thus far in my relationship life. I was just looking to make up for time I felt I had lost individually by settling down so young and being fully dedicated to only being a wife and mother. I was not looking for a commitment of any sort, but I was not turning down any fun or the ability to meet new people either. It was as if I was exhaling the old air and inhaling the new, ready to act like a brand new eighteen-year-old, picking up where I had left off before entering the relationship when I had only one child. I still was not where I wanted to be spiritually, individually, physically, or financially, but I did—without a doubt—feel that a lot of dead weight had been lifted off my shoulders, and life could not get any worse than what I had left behind. I cannot stress again, I cannot stress enough, and one more time *I cannot stress enough, how important it is* after you have had a long-term relationship with someone, to *take time* to yourself to reflect and decompress. Even if you feel you are okay because this termination is what you wanted or longed for, or if the breakup was mutual, *take some time for yourself.* It is a necessary step that is missed more times than not because we are so ready to just be done with the person we are no longer with and want to feel a sense of taking back control of our life and being an individual again.

Take the time to reflect on the relationship and who you were within that relationship. Think long and hard about what you would want to be different with the next person of your choosing, and take stock of signals or "red flags," you missed early on in meeting someone that had great potential to be compromising to yourself, needs and desires, and had contributed factors for the downfall of the relationship itself. Make a list of your needs, wants, expectations, including your deal breakers. I can guarantee you will find some behaviors to take note of, if not a whole treasure chest about yourself that you had no idea was there, which will be beneficial to your healing and moving forward in a healthy way. Disentangling from a long-term commitment of any kind and leaving what you have previously known to be your life is a lot more emotionally rattling than we'd like to admit in the freshness of that termination. It is easy to think that you feel nothing when you are numb. It is easy to fall prey to a new person in your vulnerability and loneliness to become subject to the lies of the devil mistaken as truth.

Chapter 8—It's Not Over

Have you ever had that feeling after a breakup or ending any kind of relationship that life was over, yet still beginning at the same time? After going through something that had literally brought you down to rock bottom, there was no place to go but up, and what was ahead could not be any worse than what you have already been through? Have you ever felt that whatever and whomever is in your future could not be worse than what was left behind?

In the beginning after the demise of my marriage there was a lot of chaos due to the fact that he was coming to the reality that I was no longer with him. I, myself, thought we would never come to this reality because I had faith that we would eventually arrive at a place where we were in sync. I needed to look back and evaluate. He also was dealing with a lot of trauma that was unresolved, particularly in dealing with his having been adopted. We were two broken individuals who did not unpack our baggage within, two broken and toxic people who came together in hopes of being whole together. I also identified accepting how young I was being involved with Jack and Sam and facing the fact I was taken advantage of for being so young, vulnerable and not knowing any better. Being seventeen and twenty is not mature enough psychologically to decipher if being with someone more than twice your age is appropriate for you or not. Although I did not want to be with Sam, there was still a residue of feelings that carried disappointment, a sense of failure, hurt, resentment, that I felt within myself, as well as towards him, and that I held onto. I faulted him for the individual, consistent weaknesses he contributed to the failure of the marriage. I felt he did not address my needs, or take our union seriously enough, and that together, we could just not get our marriage on track. However, I did not take the time needed to process all of what I had gone through and was still going through. In fact, I robbed myself of that time because soon after I signed the lease to the apartment where my children and I were to live, Sam was between jobs and needed a place to stay. I felt obligated to him since he was, after all, the father of my children and I allowed him to come live with us while he gained new employment and a place of his own. But I was completely unaware that I would be making another crucial mistake. I was placing his needs above mine, which would block my ability to heal and move forward. I was taking on the exact same baggage that I was so desperate to leave behind.

Not much time passed before I started spending more time with Robert. I had met him unexpectedly, so I had no expectations or thoughts that it would go past one night of hanging out and having a few drinks at a bar, which appeared to me to be very innocent.

When I met Robert there was something about his chill laid back demeanor that piqued my interest, however I originally disregarded his invitation to one day go out and have drinks. Just six months prior to meeting him I had my fourth son, Major, and one night I was sitting in the house with Sam who never paid me any attention anyway and decided why not take up Robert's offer to have a drink, so I texted him as I sat on the couch in the living room, "Ready to go have that drink?" A rush of excitement ran through my body when he responded, "I been ready." I eagerly rummaged through my closet to see what outfit I could put together and wipe the dust off my make-up kit. I did not have an occasion in a long time where it was necessary for me to get glammed up, so once I was finished, I felt like a million dollars ready to walk a red-carpet event wearing fitted blue jeans that complement the curve of my hips, a black blouse and black and white wedge Guess dress sneakers, with a silver necklace and hoop earrings. Within the hour we met, and I tailed his car as he said he had a place in mind we could go. When we arrived at the bar, the crowd was light, which I did not mind, and was glad to see darts and pool tables that filled the middle of the room in case the conversation between us became dull. I chose a table off into the corner of the bar for us to sit. As Robert sat across from me sipping his mixed patron and pineapple cocktail, I babbled away about myself and the demise of my marriage and told him about my children. The sipping of my own cocktail of patron and pineapple started to marinate within me relaxing me to a point of no mental pressure. I was focused in on spending this time with him and the voices of others in the bar was non-existent as if he and I were the only ones in the room. I did not take stock of my vulnerability. I was, in the moment, looking for a way to have some fun, and without understanding my own emotional state, I took Robert as my go-to for an escape from my reality. With Sam staying with me to watch the kids, it was convenient for me to be able to go out and spend a lot of time with Robert. I developed this outlet of escape from the responsibilities of a working, now *single* mom, who was still trying to figure it out on her own. Robert was readily available when I needed to vent about the difficulties of trying to co-parent and live with someone with whom I was no longer in a relationship.

When in the position to co-parent with an ex, the best thing you can do for the sake of your children is to put your pride to the side and the notion of always needing to prove you're right and get your point across, instead choosing the battles wisely to fight with the other parent about. A lot of children become damaged as a product of divorce when the separation is not processed in a healthy way. Although the relationship or marriage did not work out, that does not mean to rob the children of a chance to familiarize in a new normal. It is important to set expectations and consistency when possible, not putting the children in the middle to choose sides and argue and fight in front of them. The relationship is done. If it was meant to work out it would have. I found myself in that battle with Sam. I would still argue and fight with him over the reasons why I was not with him anymore, saying everything I felt when I was with him. Why keep going over and debating the same topics that were brought up during the relationship with no solution. Why not put the energy and effort to focus on the children and the best way each parent will contribute to the mental, emotional, and physical stability of the children going forward? Let the other issues go and lay down with the relationship which has officially died and just have some peace for a change. I also concluded that to keep going head-to-head with him delayed my ability to enter the healing phase because I was reaching forward with one hand, but back with the other.

Other issues on the home front were still problematic and lingering even after my mental and emotional separation. Spending time with Robert took me away from the issues in my life that I did not want to deal with when I did not want to deal with them. By the same token, it boiled down to me making my personal preferences (even before my I met Sam) which were to primarily choose only male friendships. It did not help my position that I had a secret craving for the "Good Girl, Bad Guy, Bonnie and Clyde," type of relationship which was the vibe I felt with Robert because he was a street guy. The first gun I ever saw and touched in real life was his, and my first encounter with seeing a gun being shot in the air was with him. One night we were leaving this house where Robert picked up a substantial amount of marijuana and after turning the block the police got behind my car. I knew at any moment they would switch on their lights as I drove in uneasiness making a complete stop at the stop sign and trying not to look in my rearview mirror. We were in an area known for drug dealing and after being tailed for three blocks, I am sure the police were running my plates as they closely followed behind. Eventually, they turned off to another street as I took a breath for the first time in what felt like forever. I felt a rush of adrenalin through my body for a life that I knew deep down I was not made for.

Robert was from Chicago, age forty-three at the time I met him. He had never worked a job because he hustled and sold drugs all his life, mostly heroin but whatever drug a person wanted whether it was weed, cocaine, pills etc. he was able to obtain it. The first few weeks of us being together he would leave to go to Chicago to get drugs and bring them back to Minnesota. He was what I had foolishly considered a "drug dealer with a heart." For the most part, Robert was laid back and treated everyone with respect, even the "clients" who would buy his drugs, unless and until someone crossed him. He gave me what I yearned for the most and never felt with anyone until I met him, which was security and protection. The feeling that someone had my back no matter what the situation was an overwhelming sense of safety at last—something I had never felt. He appeared to care enough to listen to all I had to say. Robert appeared to cling to my words as if his life depended on them. I felt this way because his physical and financial presence showed he was there for me no matter what. He made me feel protected and I was infatuated with his 6'2" stature, the swag he had about himself as if he were untouchable, and his deep voice that sounded like Barry White, strong enough to make the world rumble. The people in his circle seemed to have respect for him as if they knew he was the boss. Not to mention, I had all this drama around me—ranting and raving about Sam, who at this time was not technically an ex-husband, and the kids stuck in the middle. Yet still, Robert was always assuring me not only with his words, but with his actions, that he was there for me and had my "front and my back," as he would say, always ready to embrace me with open arms. He became to me what I felt was the best friend I never had.

When we were together, we had a great time and there was no pressure. It felt organically natural. I had just met this person, yet it seemed like I knew him from before. I felt dead for so many years and with him I felt resurrected and thought *this is what I've been missing*. At this point, I was not considering Robert as anything more than a friend, but then when we became sexually intimate, he became a best friend with what I thought were great "benefits" because of his loyalty to me. Now this new "arrangement" for me was not so bad since my initial thoughts were not on being in a relationship after ten years in one that had drained every ounce of me and was now a failed marriage under my belt. In the beginning I just set out to have fun and go with the flow. I had no intentions of opening the door to my heart and catching any romantic feelings anytime soon, while trying to pick up the pieces of my life, unsure where it was headed next. Once again, I was in a situation where I was not completely physically attracted, but Robert had the swag to make up for the physical imperfections I was able to overlook, and he held me in such high regard where I had never been held before. He made me feel that I was the most important person to him, and I had never had this feeling from anyone. I was important to him. He needed me. I'd spent so many years making someone else the center of my life, and now finally, the tables had been flipped and I was the priority.

When Robert came into the picture, I felt the timing could not had been more perfect. I wanted him in my life forever and I never could have imagined life without him. This was, for sure, a lifelong friendship, connection, attachment—whatever I wanted to call it at that time. He was here for me. And he was not going anywhere. He was the first person that I felt really loved me at this point. And he had no expectations but for me to allow him to be a part of my life.

As the months went on and the fairy dust settled, the relationship with Robert still had its moments of fun, but I started to see he possessed some toxic traits and then I saw them also in myself, and in us together. What brought us together, hanging out, and drinking, was our foundation. We would go out to the clubs, take ecstasy pills and smoke weed. Then the feeling of always wanting to be with him began to shift its course, and it was not what it had started off. I went from wanting to spend every moment I could make available to him, to being with him a week then needing a break from him to then within a few days I was tired of him. The lines between our "situationship," became blurry because it was a mixture of being "friends" not in a committed relationship but living as if we were in a relationship. I was committed to him in a way because at this point I had already invested a bit of time, but I still was searching for something Robert did not seem to fulfill in the long term, so I met other people and went on other dates here and there. But it seemed that even trying to have a moment of fun outside of Robert, I was not getting the same energy from the other guys, Because of that, I was held in a stance that I could not get better than what Robert had to offer. The chemistry we had could not be matched and felt like a once in a lifetime opportunity. Back in the dating world after over ten years, I felt it had changed, and for me, it was not for the better. So I found myself running into different people that I ultimately realized were a complete waste of my time. Robert made it difficult for guys to compete because of how he treated me. I began to pick up vibes that Robert was not the vision I had for myself in the long term, so there was a part of me now that was desperate to look for those qualities that he did not possess in other men. I struggled, teeter-tottering in my indecisive mind with maybe trying to make it work with Robert in a committed relationship because I loved him. But in a desperate attempt to fix my love life, I tried something new and entered the online dating life.

Instantly I met someone. He was attractive, he possessed goals and ambitions, he was looking to settle down and have a wife, having spent several years of his life in the marines. On paper everything lined up for what I was looking for. After talking for a few days, we met each other at my job on Christmas. He was more attractive in person than he was in his pictures, told me God was the center of his life, and within the last year his mother had passed. He was pleasant, articulate, and spoke like he was sure of himself and had a good head on his shoulders. The finishing touch was when, out of nowhere and with no prompting, unbeknown to him, he put on one of my favorite gospel songs, "God Favored Me" by Hezekiah Walker. It was in that instant I felt this was the man that God sent to me. Although I was not getting "butterflies" in my stomach or a genuine feeling of confirmation in my spirit, I felt it couldn't be a coincidence that he played that song. Over the next few days we continued to speak and then there was a transformation. I was starting not to take his words as golden as they were sold to me because his actions were not lining up and I told him I did not want to speak to him again. I felt this way because he never asked me questions about myself to get to know me better. He never asked about my children even though I told him I had them. There was not any effort to take me out on a date or so much to know what was my favorite food or color. Unless I was asking him a question, he only talked about himself and his life.

When I got off work that night it was snowing, and I had not yet put a brush and ice-scraper in my car. As I was walking through the parking lot, I saw him smiling ear to ear as he was dusting off my car with nothing but a long sleeve sweater and vest. Now I am thinking in my mind once again this is another confirmation of who this man who is going to be there for me, because another thing I had decided I needed from a man was that he would show initiative and effort to prove to me that it mattered if I was around or not. Yet even with the song and the pop up of dusting the snow off my car, something in my spirit did not sit right. Every time after we would speak over the phone, my spirit was uneasy and my heart was literally ready to jump out of my chest, and not in a good way. My soul was heavy and if that intuitive flash of fire in my chest was not a sign, I do not know what else it could have been. I had prayed on it; in fact, this was the first time I had ever prayed and consulted with God over a potential relationship, and these feelings would not go away.

The next evening when we met with each other something in my mind in the middle of conversation prompted me to ask him what my name was. He could not even say it. Instead he replied by saying he knew my name. I literally felt my heart drop to the floor. It was as if my body completely deflated. This person who told me that I am someone he wanted to spend his life with and told me he was "all in," could not even tell me my name! I simply got out of his car and walked away. I was so caught up in certain qualities of knowing what I did and did not want, it just about took over my whole spirit of discernment and the way God was giving me confirmation of what I knew did not appear to be all that was presented. In situations like this, where God shows us what to do and what is what, we sometimes still question when God has already given us the answer. We sometimes go back to God, asking, "but are you sure?" Or we may try to reason with God, as if he were a God who would lie to us and does not already know the outcomes we do not see. I would date thinking and looking that this next guy I meet had to be the one for me. This is when I was first introduced to "gas-lighting" and "love bombing." It also alerted me to something new. Although I did like this man, I was insanely attracted to him, but because I was not sexually intimate with him, there were not any soul ties to be broken, so even though it was disappointing, I was able to walk away from the situation without a broken heart, and it was as if it had never happened. It was also a realization that just because a man says he is "of God," does not mean he is the man for you and how necessary it is to be careful about "leaping before looking." We can connect with God, allowing Him to be the guide to direct our path and we can pray for a spirit of discernment and for confirmation.

After being disappointed and discouraged yet again and because I am still human, I unconsciously moved back into what was familiar to me. Time passed and issues between Robert and me started to become physically abusive where he was putting his hands on me or I was putting my hands on him. At times, I began to see slight traits of jealousy. Not only in him but in me as well. I told him about some of the dates I went on, but he accused me of more than just going out for dates. I also accused him of things with other women and I would go through his phone while he was sleeping and it would confirm he was talking to other women or sending what I thought to be inappropriate texts to the mother of his children. But I doubted he was involved with anyone else because we spent so much time together or on the phone, and when I went over to his house unexpectedly, I was never confronted with him and any other women. I was stuck in a place of attempting to keep my two worlds separate. He was good enough for me to escape my realities and responsibilities, but I did not feel right when he entered my day-to-day life. My spiritual stance, being a mother who understood the sacrifices that come with parenting, going to work and taking care of my responsibilities and the path I knew I did ultimately aspire to, which was to stand in the plans that God had for every part of my life, differed from Robert's desires and the path he wanted for his life. I did not have the aspiration firmly in my heart to have a future with Robert, although many times I had thought about settling with him because it was hard for me to grasp enough faith that God had someone specifically set aside for me. At the same time, it was crushing for me emotionally and mentally to think of Robert being with someone else, even though I did not wholly want him. When we started to fight with each other, we never knew how quickly a night of going out for fun would end up in an argument. With a flip of the coin we could end up in each other's arms at the end of the evening, or a major volcano might erupt between us. We would go weeks without talking after a major blow up, then one of us would initiate speaking again and we would get back together as if nothing had happened.

Then one day I believe God sent me an intervention to escape the relationship with Robert. We had a big argument the night before but the next morning I woke up with a calm mental state and decided to call him; his phone went straight to voicemail. After attempting the call again, I thought that was odd because of the work he did, Robert never powered off his phone. A few hours later I received a pre-paid call from him in jail. I remember being distraught and felt guilty that I could not remember what we were fighting about the evening before and how it wasn't worth whatever it was we fought about if either of us had known he would be in jail the next day. I took off work so that I could attend his court hearing and see him. Standing behind a glass in an orange jumpsuit with a deputy behind him, his demeanor did not appear to be scared but it was more so an expression of "displacement." His bond was originally set for $500,000 then reduced to $50,000 and he was able to bond out while he went through the motions of his case.

Robert had gone to a CVS the morning he was arrested to get hygiene items such as soap and toothpaste and said when he walked out the store the parking lot was filled with officers and a canine dog and the officers were yelling for him to get on the ground. He said that he was taken aback and froze in his steps thinking, "This has to be a dream," so initially he just stood in the revolving doors of the store. As I sat on his bed and read the court documents tears ran down my face. For a month, July to August, he had been set up by a drug user he sold drugs to in a sting operation. Over the course of that month when the person was buying heroin from Robert, he was requesting larger amounts and the police were watching and documenting the transactions. Robert was able to convince the court that he also was a drug user and not a drug dealer in the pursuit to get less time, as he was sentenced to a drug court to provide nonviolent drug-addicted offenders treatment. He was ordered two months in jail and ten years' probation. While he was in jail, I spoke to him one time when another argument ensued between us, and for the rest of his time I ignored his calls in an attempt to ween myself from him. However, the day he was released I felt the need to see him and we picked up where we left off.

Outside of this relationship with Robert, life was finally evolving a bit for me personally. I was able to secure a job as a bus operator that allowed me to be able to take care of my children, pay my bills more consistently, pay off debts that were left after separating from my ex, and I was in a position where I was able to buy a home that my children and I could call ours, as we were living in a cramped two-bedroom apartment. I felt stuck in muddy waters, and all that had weighed me down and was still weighing me down. Yet, I felt I was moving forward if only inch by inch.

I was in a constant battle with myself over living in sin and being weak in my flesh, allowing my mind and emotions to overpower me, crushed by the pains of my past and wondering how and why certain people did not fit into the lives of my children. I was feeling Robert was my personal safety net at times, and yet I knew what I wanted for a healthy relationship— and I knew that he fell short. I asked myself what would be the breaking point to decide and stop see-sawing back and forth? Would there ever be a breaking point?

Being stuck in survival mindset, it is hard to relax. Your mind is always worrying and wondering about the future or what is going to happen in the next second. How to be prepared for all the "what ifs" is not easy when you are living life on the edge. As I continued to allow my life to be intertwined with more distractions, I felt my heart was always getting broken left or right. I was beginning to feel bitter as the matters between Robert and I were getting worse. The toxicity of our chemistry was now obvious and the unsettling spirit in me started to overwhelm me. But I was still scared to move on despite what I felt.

Once gifted with the insight of being "gaslighted" and "love bombed," I was skeptical of who might be meant for me to share my life with. Did I even deserve to have love? I was broken and wondered with all my built-up trauma; did I have the capacity to love someone properly? Would I ever be able to receive love without having to question its authenticity? I did not have family and I did not have any friends outside of Robert, somewhat by choice because of my trust issues. It was hard for me to connect with people and put myself out there. I was not looking for someone perfect, just someone who was perfect for me. I was stuck in thinking I would never connect with anyone like Robert again on a romantic or friendship level. Stuck trying to make him realize I was the prize to be won, feeling like I did with my ex-husband. I thought I could barter to let go of some characteristics, some of the things I wanted, if he would just be a certain kind of man with some of the qualities I was looking for. Here I was knee-deep again in what was familiar to me because the fear of the unknown was too uncomfortable. The wave of emotions I went through felt unbearable when I tried to stop talking to him. I was not comfortable being completely alone and wanted some type of companionship at the expense of pulling me away from God and leading me to sin. If you stay in sin to have it, you will stay in sin to keep it. He was not completely meeting my needs, not feeding my soul, nor making me happy because I needed that instant gratification. There were eerie similarities with Robert that aligned with the reasons I did not want my marriage to continue, and all the relationships before that. I could not come to terms with how hard it was to let go of the men that I knew were not good for me, or even someone I knew I did not intend to have a long-term romantic connection with. I confounded myself trying to analyze what was so difficult when I had the ability to cut other people out my life for much less. Matters had escalated to the worst end of the spectrum with Robert because I was wrapped up in being concerned if he were to be with anyone else other than me, especially sexually. I had reached the state that is described as, "Don't want 'em, but don't want nobody else to have 'em," despite the nagging feeling that I would still feel incomplete choosing to be with him. There were zero accountability points for his actions and choices in his life and he chose to say, unapologetically, *Take me as I am, I have always been this way, and I am not changing for anyone.*

If a man does not want to be better for himself or his own children, why would he want to be better for you or for your children that are not even his? Accountability forces you to look at yourself and the role that you play specifically taking anyone else out the equation. To dig into your shortcomings, missteps, and look at your own responsibility can be a tough pill to swallow which is why a lot of people choose to ignore what is at hand. It is always easier to point the finger at others, but while you are busy pointing, how many fingers are you willing to point towards yourself?

Robert began to be more verbally abusive and disrespectful in the way he spoke to me, and by the way he treated me so that I no longer felt that it mattered if we were in each other's lives. I believe at this point he felt I was so emotionally invested that after three years; I was not going anywhere and I was "hooked." He used the conversations of me wanting more and knowing in the long haul what I did and did not want for life, and the lives of my children, against me as tactics of manipulation to make me feel as though my expectations were too high, although I knew deep down my motives were pure. My life and outlook had evolved from when we first started, and I was not in the same space mentally, although physically I could not get myself to move. Now, instead of being my biggest cheerleader, Robert downplayed my efforts to make life better for my children and myself and rubbed my aspirations in the mud. It was unsettling but I continued to allow myself to be pulled back in, time and time again, because of my fear of what the unknown future held. I would say I was done with my own way of doing things and put in motion an effort to get closer to God, to be still, have faith, be away from Robert four or five weeks—but then I could no longer fight the urge to see him. I would get off track and discouraged by my own way of thinking, setting myself up again to believe that things between us were not as bad as I made up in my mind, and that we could somehow still co-exist with each other because of the history that we had. I am here to say it loudly in your ear, *It does not matter how long you have known someone, if they are not good for you, then that is that.*

There is no dancing around that revelation to make it go from dark to light. Life does not wait just because someone has been around you X number of years in your life. I could not grasp how someone who was not in any way good for me, not elevating me, not adding value to my life, could still draw me in. A soul tie is when you have an attachment to another individual physically, emotionally, mentally, and/or spiritually that can be detrimental to your well-being. In my own ignorance I had developed a soul tie, a soul tie that was ungodly. This soul tie can be strongly enforced especially after sexual intercourse has been involved. There is a sense of commitment to the connection with this person that makes it difficult to let them go. Whenever you decide to lay down and give your body to another person there is an exchange of energy fields with each other that creates a bonding. It can be seen as the same when you are leery of someone coming into your home because you have a sense that their spirit is off, and you do not want to invite that energy into your home. Soul ties are very real. They offer a lesson to be learned for the sin we have pursued and have allowed into our life. *Stop allowing the enemy a way in the door!* It is so important to build relationships that are worth building, those which fuel you and do not deplete you. Those who support you, respect and love you and help build your God-given purpose.

CHAPTER 9—JUST STOP RUNNING

Choices can be made in love, but that love can be derived from—and rooted in—how we see ourselves, our childhood, past experiences or what we have witnessed in our lives regarding others. I knew I wanted love, but there is a difference when you know you are deserving of love. It is one thing to say you are a worthy individual, but it is another to walk as if you truly believe and know and are unmoved to settle for less than you deserve. Why take just the horse when you can have the horse with the carriage, when you can have spacious room packed with great things and not just be taken for a ride.

On a Friday, against my better judgement, I felt that it would be innocent to have a night out with Robert after again attempting to distance myself from him a few weeks prior. I felt that I was stable now and that it would be harmless because I was cemented in taking the relationship for what it was, as it was. Before we could even begin our date, we had yet another huge war, about the same issue regarding our different views on life and our different paths in each other's lives. My goal was to never belittle him. Like with Sam it was to encourage personal development that you can be better despite the circumstances. I couldn't deliver a message to someone who didn't want to receive it. The next day he was so angry with me, he cussed me out. I was disrespected beyond belief and abused beyond any way he had ever treated me. My faith and spirituality were attacked. I was verbally attacked on my stance as a woman. I was also personally dumbfounded. I had just gotten off of work and was driving home, pulling into my garage and letting the door down with the engine still running and my windows drawn up. Yet I could smell the fumes of the exhaust seeping in. He said to me, "Stop crying, remember you're God's only child so you are stronger than that. God don't help nobody but you. It's all about you. You're the only one who went to college and bought a home and went through any struggle. If you lived in Chicago and came from where I did you wouldn't make it through one day. You're not like those West Side Chicago girls." With a great degree of force he yelled into the phone, "this is how I am and if anyone doesn't like it, they don't have to be around me. This is my life and I choose to live it how I want. If I want to mess it up, that's what I'm going to do because don't nobody do anything for me." With raging anger Robert threatened to shoot me in my face, and bust my face with a bat. I sat on the phone with him for almost an hour flooded with uncontrollable tears because I did not want him in my life any longer under any circumstance. I felt foolish for trickling back and I was sick and tired of being sick and tired. Because my emotions were so unbearable, I couldn't go into the house with my kids to see me so distraught and broken down. They were old enough to recognize when anything was not okay with me and I didn't want my children to question my emotional state. After his chaotic ranting, getting what he felt needed off of his chest, revealing his authentic colors and true state of mind, he hung the phone up in my face. I turned the engine off to my car and sat and collected myself until I could at least stop the tears from falling from my eyes.

When I got to my bedroom which I painted pink, symbolizing my favorite color, also to soothe me in my room, and to reach the inner child who never had that bedroom glamorized in girly decor, I literally fell onto my knees and cried out to Jesus from everything in my heart, to the pit of my soul and every inch of my being that I wanted to live my life for Jesus and I asked for forgiveness and surrendered all. I no longer wanted to be tied to anything or anyone that wasn't right for me and I only desired what God wanted and intended for my life. I was also angry and disturbed with myself that I'd sat there and listened to a man, whom I thought loved me, belittle and degrade me. Robert's ultimate and authentic characteristics came out that night and there was no mistaken who he was. And that is what he was always going to be. After over four and a half years of my involvement with Robert and all that came with it, I had finally come to a realistic and spiritual crossroads to make the decision that I did not want to ride the roller coaster with him any longer. That I did not want to live a life that was not pleasing to God, even if it meant being completely alone, uncomfortable, along with anything and everything else that was in God's plans for my life that I did not envision for myself. The gut-wrenching pain I had was the conviction I needed. It was like I was going to keep being replayed in the same scene every time I went back to where God did not want me to be and not make any change. It was like watching a movie over and over; you want a different ending, but you already know how it is going to play out. The same way it has when you watched it fifty times before. It appeared as if everything I ever wanted or felt I wanted was stripped from me. A mother/daughter relationship. The daughter I longed to have after having my fourth son. The marriage I put everything into to work. The external family that I had been born into that however never felt like family. Robert, the first man who I felt truly loved me and would never do anything to hurt me knowing what I had already been through. The associates that appeared would lead to life-long friendships. Ripped! See the keywords? "I ever wanted." It was not what God wanted because He knew all the parts that I could not see and could not fix upon in my frame of thinking.

On that September evening, I chose to rededicate my life to God and allow him to take the wheel in every way possible. Have you ever had a toothbrush that you felt so connected with? That this toothbrush was the toothbrush of a lifetime, and you would not find one that worked or felt any better? You want to move on and throw out the old one, you have even made the effort, at least, to go out and purchase a new one, in fact you have accumulated several new toothbrushes. Although the toothbrush you are using is old, raggedy, the color has faded, the bristles are falling off, it still feels good despite not working to its full capacity. You only stick with it because it is familiar.

Afraid of embarking on a new wave, making new memories, new milestones because it had been comfortable where I was, and it is what I knew from the beginning, I knew that severing ties with Robert would not come without difficulty. But I was not prepared for the transition I was set to experience. God had me in motion to experience the breakthrough of a lifetime. Although I had placed myself in a situation not of God, he used this brokenness to open the floodgates to much needed healing.

I was faced with an alarm and I needed to respond to it. I was crushed mentally, emotionally, and spiritually and told God I had nothing else left to give. I was uncomfortable but felt an unrecognizable peace within me. Then God placed me in a position to purge me of anything that was not of Him because I became isolated. I literally had no one around me or anyone to talk to but God and my children. Certain messages became evident that God wanted me to receive because they kept coming up. I would log onto YouTube to watch a video sermon and faith would keep coming up. Or harboring unforgiveness was the subject of the sermons I would randomly choose. Or relationships and distractions. These messages seemed to speak directly to me and what I was going through. I had never heard of Jerry Flowers, and stumbled upon him as if randomly, but there was a purpose in what I heard. There was Tony Gaskin and RC Blakes. Before my only go to would be Joyce Meyers. She is wonderful as well, but where I was now in my life, God wanted to invite me to hear a different delivery of messages. God will use different people and situations to get you where He wants you to be. An airplane flies you where you need to go, but that aircraft may not be the same one you get on after your layover on the way to your trip.

A few weeks prior to this happening I was cleaning my room and as I bent over to get the trash bag out the can, I heard the spirit tell me, "I'm getting ready to do something new." God was getting ready to clean house with me. Things in life had already begun to shift out of what I knew. After four years of allowing my ex-husband to stay with me for the sake of the kids and trying to help him while he got his stuff together, I told him enough was enough, that helping him was coming at the expense of my peace, happiness, and growth. Whether he had a place or not, he needed to figure it out, but he could no longer stay with me because I was ready to fully close the chapter with him. I finally came to the realization that I was delaying my ability to heal wholly and move on from what came of the relationship with my ex-husband and me.

A few months prior to me telling him he could no longer stay with me; our divorce was finalized. The day I said, "I do," there were all types of alarm bells going off, not to mention it took seven years for us to get to this point, having his family play on my phone and harass me just hours after getting married. There was never a sense of a real marriage commitment and covenant, so I never took his last name. Therefore I did not see a sense of urgency to get the wheels moving in a divorce proceeding. However, in a way I felt that not getting it done kept me connected to him. Certainly, allowing him to stay in my home for those four years had been an impediment to my true independence. In the process of the divorce, I petitioned the court for a full legal name change. I wanted to rid myself of the family name I was given, because I knew that I did not want to be attached to that legacy either. There was a lot of unresolved trauma and secrets within the family I came from on my mother's side, and although I did not know exactly what all that was about, I knew that I was destined and called to be a generational curse breaker. I wanted to confront my demons and not just bury them in a closet. Amid my chaos and things shifting upward with the emotional, mental, and spiritual truth of "growth hurts," God was showing me that new things were brewing for me. There were choices that I needed to make because I felt my circumstances had boiled down literally to a matter of life or death for me. I finally refused to stay in dysfunction. And I had a mustard seed of faith to embark on this new walk, the best thing that could ever happen to me. To walk in Christ became a matter of my relationship with God, trusting Him with every part of my being, the morals, and values I truly believed in, breaking the negative thoughts I had of myself, overcoming the fear of the future, healing from my past traumas, striving for better, and severing old habits.

Even with all I had been through in life, I never was as broken and shattered to pieces as I was in that moment. This was the first time I had ever experienced letting go of someone whom I was not in love with but still genuinely had love for and cared about which made this path difficult for me to navigate, even if I had strong convictions that it was for the best in the long run. If the person or people you are giving your time to are not capable of keeping up with your journey towards wholeness, your purpose and kingdom vibes, helping to build your momentum—then that is a distraction holding you back from your true path.

Everybody is not meant and cannot go to the next level to which God is bringing you. I beat myself up for a long time for not knowing how to discern these different types of relationships that ended with the same results, leaving me feeling broken down and unappreciated. There was a period when I regretted the time I felt went wasted, feeling lost and confused, not realizing the problem lay within myself, even if a man was not who he said he was, or who I thought I could make him be. I internalized guilt for not being in tune with myself to realize and know that I was wasting my time earlier on. However I came to a clear conscience that no experience is ever truly wasted, because through everything there was something that had to be learned and that was God's way of doing it, because He is so faithful He meets us where we are. I was vulnerable, in fact even gullible, because the people I had encountered up until this point appeared as loving when they ultimately were not. Yet I had yearned for love so badly because I wanted a loving attachment so badly.

Those of us who have not come from homes or families where love is genuinely felt and expressed are more likely to stay in unloving relationships because of the neediness and the desire to feel needed. I wanted to be treated like a respected person. I wanted to be treated well and not just be the girl with the "nice shape," because I knew I was more than that. I knew deep down that I was a child of God. A Queen and Daughter of a King, I had a deep desire to form connections to those with whom I could praise God. I sought a friend whom I could trust to laugh and cry with me. I wanted people around me whom I could pray for and pray with, who wanted to be in alignment with Jesus as much as I did. There was a desire to be picked up for a date and not be the chauffeur. To have flowers given to me not because of an occasion. For doors to be opened for me and my chair pulled out for me, welcoming me at a surprise romantic dinner. To feel safe and protected. To be able to wholeheartedly trust without doubt and fear trolling my every step. To have the courage to wait on what God specifically ordained for me. I craved that need for change. I craved for God to come full circle in my heart and heal my brokenness. I knew that I would never be perfect, but I was always trying to make progress and to mirror my life in Christ. I was tired of getting in my own way and being the cause of my own downfall, the heartbreaks and brokenness. As I stated in the very beginning, ultimately the choice is yours despite where you have started and what life has thrown at you.

I was doing the work needed to get my life on track on the outside but what was I investing inwardly? Why was I still coming up with a depreciated value? Insecurity can have you questioning every aspect of your being and choices and you can find yourself easily filled with anxiety and self-torment. At this point for the first time ever—I could not even trust my own thoughts and decisions. Even if I was not evolving as quickly as I wanted, or in the way I wanted—never mind that it felt like pulling teeth without Novocain— I evolved eventually, nevertheless.

A lot of times you will feel defeated and lose faith but your desire for becoming better must be stronger than your current circumstances. It is like being sick from food poisoning when your body goes through the motions of sickness to eject the poisonous contents from your body. You are not better immediately but after you begin to be able to feed yourself with nourishment and become rehydrated you are in motion to become your better self. No matter what I was faced with, the grace of God and His Holy Spirit would always be my way back to my foundation of belief and that is what kept me persevering spiritually and mentally. With the people I found myself wrapped in, both past and present, there was a pattern of trying to remold me into a person I did not desire to be in any way, shape, or form, for the worse and not for the better.

Take a moment. Write down a list of the people in your life whom you consider close or whom you interact with on almost a daily basis. You can even write down characteristics of yourself. There is one question to be asked—is he/she/it adding to your life or subtracting from it? There are no buts or explanations. It is simply an addition or subtraction sign, a plus or a minus. If a person or a characteristic you have listed has a minus sign , it is time to evaluate your stance in that relationship moving forward with that person or with that characteristic within yourself.

I was on an emotional roller coaster that I did not enjoy but still climbed into for another ride, time and again. While I was healing, the love I had for Robert devolved from despising him to feeling disgust about him, then regret, and finally hatred. I played my role inserting myself in this relationship, but I had also placed blame on him feeling that he ruined my life because my feet seemed to be cemented into this need for him. Those feelings turned into unforgiveness and pity for myself for putting myself in such a situation, and dealing with the consequences of my choices emotionally, mentally, and spiritually. I became regretful of the times I'd neglected some of my priorities, the many times I sacrificed time that I could have spent with my children instead of sharing my time with him. I felt selfish. It is the disappointment of loving someone who does not reciprocate and is incapable of loving you back that is hurtful. It was the repetitive effort to pick myself up from the shattered pieces of life once again and attempt to redefine myself and find my identity. It was the going back to the beginning, which I felt I'd never left, where my own mother did not and would not love me. Every hurt I had suffered was coming to the surface for me to address at full speed, even people and events that I thought I was not affected by. This type of hurt literally pierces your soul. You feel it deep down in your stomach. How is that even possible when your heart is in your chest? I also acknowledged along the way that pieces of my faith had been stripped away with every counterfeit man I encountered.

When I was pregnant with my fourth child, I prayed and believed with everything in me and knew for certain I was having a daughter. I had brought nothing but girls' clothing. I even had a girl's name picked out. I even had a dream I was holding a baby girl in my arms, and then I woke to my reality on September 1st that I was indeed having another son. I knew God knew how much I desired to have a daughter. What it would mean to me—because I had prayed so many times about it, pouring out my heart that I needed a daughter so I could have the relationship with her I never had with my mother. I thought that having a daughter would fix a lot, if not all, of the problems I was facing within. I was always running after the antidote to solve the problem, running again, then running some more. I did not know what it was like to be "Still." Many times, in life we are asking God to show us the way when all He wants us to do is to be Still and walk in faith.

Although I wish I had bypassed the "journey lessons," in some ways God used those exact situations to put me in a position where the only place I could run was into his arms and his presence because I had nothing left of myself to give. God placed me in a position where I never felt so dire and desperate to respond, to take the time to cleanse my heart, mind, body, and soul. He wanted my full attention. This was something that I had never done or tried until this point. Many times, we are skipping a class that is necessary and when the graduation ceremony comes, our lack of eligibility to be on the stage because of the class that was skipped was the exact class needed to advance. The missed class gives us the feeling of vulnerability, lack of control, inadequacy, fearful feelings, brings pressures and challenges to confront what we have kept buried and hidden from anyone else to see. There are times we are going to the class then skipping out because of the distractions in the hallway. The noise, the sound of "fun," the thinking the grass was greener on the playground causing us to ditch our lessons and our homework. If you want something different you must do something different. My mind frame was no longer on the life I wanted or envisioned for myself.

I no longer set my sights on hanging out with people just to hang or to worry about who did not want to do and be better or surrounding myself with unmotivated people who were not hungry for God to transform their lives and settle their personal demons. It had nothing to do with being humble or thinking I was any higher or better than others. I knew a shift in my life was forming and the things of the past and the people that came with it were due to completely expire and fall away. Robbers do not break into empty homes. I cried a lot and at times I did not even know why I was crying. This was different from everything I had ever experienced up to this point in my life. It was the releasing of all that I had bottled up, hid, and held back and ignored. The pain, the trauma, the disappointments, the offenses, the feelings of being counted out and not good enough—then the realization that being rejected, belittled, and spoken down to, as well as the fake friendships and the loveless relationships—these were the best things that could have happened to me because the pain pushed me to the brink of where I needed to be, which was tired of my own stuff.

I remember one morning spending time with Jesus on my bed in stillness looking out my window and I could see that it was drizzling outside but the sun was still beaming. The spirit told me there was beauty and sunshine even in the rain. God has an ordained a destiny for you to follow and do not allow others to attempt to make you feel guilty for wanting to receive all that God has in store for you. I had to learn it was okay to do what was best for me and step onto the journey I wanted to be on. Even if it meant standing alone. I wanted to be where God wanted me to be. It comes to a point where your spirit literally gets tired of being in relationships and positions that do not fulfill your soul or serve your purpose. No matter what you do or how you go about it, there is still an emptiness felt inside. God never said that He would not help you through it. The question is: have you even tried to turn to God to see what He will do? You are not equipped to carry the load by yourself without failing. That is where supernatural strength and power is needed, which no human on earth carries. Most times we are fighting a war that is not for us but we ourselves choose to take it on, adding fuel to a fire we did not start but have helped to inflame.

A good indication you are surrendering to God is that you feel very uncomfortable and battle different waves of emotions. This path of hurt is what I call, "Soul Changing Hurt." That kind of hurt is the beginning of new life brewing. The pressure always builds when it is about to break. Then it's time to release because the pressure can no longer be contained. All is being prepared for you, all that God has in store for you. You are walking into where God wants you to be. You can fight the pressure and create a mess, or you can allow the pressure to come through and burst into a nice flow. The choice is yours. It is time to choose!

I understand when you are trying to smile through tears and sadness to secretly put away the face of emotions of how you really feel for your children, those you love, your friends, co-workers, when you feel like you are drowning and dying inside. It's okay. Continue pushing past that heartfelt pain, those will be temporary feelings because there is a better life, a better *you* will develop. *Guaranteed.*

However, the work to do is up to you and only you can do it. There is a craving for you to have peace, healing, wholeness, liberty, and it is natural to avoid the work you need to invest to secure those positions. But the treasure can only be found if you are digging in the right space. The only ones who receive the real award are the ones who put in the work. When I began to really dedicate my walk with God, I began to hear his voice much clearer allowing myself to be more in alignment with Him. Even when I did not understand or it was uncomfortable, when I felt like giving up, when I was hurting, when I was having moments of weakness, struggling with the things I wanted to change outwardly and inwardly. God wants it all. God wants you in all your moments, in all your brokenness so he can bring healing to all of you. I have been there and believe me when I say that those feelings are indeed temporary. God even said trouble does not last, does not go on forever. "And after you have suffered a little while, the God of all grace [Who imparts all blessing and favor], Who has called you to His [own] eternal glory in Christ Jesus, will Himself complete and make you what you ought to be, establish and ground you securely, and strengthen, and settle you." "(1 Peter5:10) (AMPC). ""That weeping may endure for a night, but joy comes in the morning." "(Psalm 30:5)"

First, I needed to assess and address what weakness it was that was causing me to feel so stuck. The healing starts with what a lot of people don't want to do, which is to open the cluttered closet, the one where everything is stuffed in so that when you open it everything just comes tumbling out. It begins with cataloging what you went through starting at the beginning, with your childhood which began to shape you. In my case, no one had ever showed me that they cared even just a little bit where I could feel it, therefore, I was vulnerable to that feeling of care even if it were toxic. Bleeding and busted up, how many times are you going to keep ramming yourself into a wall? When will enough actually be enough? The devil will try to use your weakness to keep you trapped. Although satan is evil, he can still know your thoughts and patterns. The weakness of wanting to be loved, to be with someone, to have someone care for you and someone you can care for, can keep you in relationships that God does not want you to be in. You need first to realize God is all you need, despite what you may feel or what you are going through. The feeling of wanting to be needed and not to feel alone kept me in toxic relationships, even when I realized how toxic they became, and that was not the life I wanted to continue to live in. The devil fought me harder. Fight the devil with the same tools he is trying to use against you to keep you in bondage. When you are not afraid to be alone, he cannot use that against you. If you have no fear because you are standing firm in knowing that God is always with you and for you, the devil cannot use fear against you. When you walk confidently knowing that God has given you all the love you could ever need, the devil will flee from you. It has nothing to do with the other person. It has everything to do with you.

Ephesians 6:11 (AMPC) reminds us, "Put on God's whole armor [the armor of a heavy-armed soldier which God supplies], that you may be able successfully to stand up against all the strategies and the deceits of the devil." Remember that word accountability we spoke about? It hurts for me to see us, as God's children in bondage, so imagine how God feels. He wants to be there for you, but you must allow him in wholeheartedly. The devil would not be fighting you so hard if God did not have a seed of purpose and a plan for your life. Jeremiah 29:11: "For I know the thoughts and plans that I have for you, says the Lord, thoughts and plans for welfare and peace and not for evil, to give you hope in your final outcome." Trust in God, rely on God, lean into God. Stop right now entertaining the foolishness you do not want to have in your space in exchange for what you truly desire and deserve. God will pull you out of the fire and there will be no scars or residue.

The battle in your mind between your spirituality, qualities, and the morals that you stand by and believe in is a good indication a red flag is waving and you are somewhere you should not be. You should not have to question or compromise between right and wrong actions. For example, say that you are a law-abiding citizen, and you are dealing with someone who deems no relation of their actions to the consequences. You are unevenly yoked. Darkness and light cannot coexist together. Ephesians 5:11 (AMPC) tells us, "Take no part in and have no fellowship with the fruitless deeds and enterprises of darkness." Do not keep allowing an entry for something that God is trying to break away from you, something that is keeping you stuck, from healing, keeping you from building a firm foundation with God. A decision must be made; both feet in or both feet out. It was only by God's grace that He broke me from relationships I wanted to be free of but I had seen no way through because I felt that the entanglements of my past and my negative characteristics had a strong hold over me. I know what I felt was more than what I could have brought myself out of alone because I tried so many times and failed in my own strength. It was only when I had a sincere desire to be free and wholeheartedly wanted to be one with Christ that I began to see the change in my spirit. I felt as if I was in recovery. I noticed I was laughing authentically and organically for the first time ever in my life. I felt a sense of peace no matter what was going on. I was learning to recognize the schemes of the enemy to take me back where I had been and to identify the thoughts that tried to derail my progress. I was genuinely enjoying my children more than I had ever done before. I no longer had a desire to fornicate. I no longer allowed myself to succumb to a glass filled half with fear and half with doubt. I no longer worried if God would bring me a spouse to share my life with. There are times when you pray and what you feel is overwhelming and what you are dealing with is constantly gnawing at you—that is the time to leave it all at The Lord's feet.

There is also a conscience needed to oversee that the things we are asking for God to manifest do not become idols. I constantly prayed for a husband, so much so I felt that until a husband appeared, I could not be happy. I allowed that neediness to affect my life and it was blocking my gratitude to God for all that He had done for me before. I was so wrapped up in wanting a husband that the Holy Spirit revealed that I was putting my desire for a husband above God so much it had, indeed, become an idol. When the Holy Spirit speaks to me, it mostly comes in the form of a quiet intimate voice speaking directly to me, followed by confirmation, with biblical truths. Some people may have dreams or visions by the Holy Spirit.

The feeling is a full circle of peace within and clarity, which allows me to know where I am getting it wrong in the way I'm proceeding. In a sense I had drowned out God's voice because I was not focusing on my relationship with Him first. I just wanted Him to deliver the husband stamped and approved with expedited shipping.

When your focus is more on the gifts then that of the Giver, your lines are crossed and your true needs need to be reassigned. Matthew 6:33 (NLT) says, "Seek the Kingdom of God above all else, and live righteously, and he will give you everything you need." He knows the desire of your heart and yes, He wants you to ask and tell Him, knock, seek and you shall find, but this is also about one of the most important steps we miss and that is believing that He will take care of all.

You do not have to take the longest road of the journey. There will be times that the journey will be long but there are ways to minimize the wear and tear. You have the insight to be and do better and it all starts with God and yourself because everything that can happen in your life flows from those two things. God, of course, comes first. Apart from God, we can do nothing. "John 15:5 NIV; says "I am the vine; you are the branches. If you remain in me and I in you, you will bear much fruit; apart from me you can do nothing." I had a physical example of this one summer when I needed to cut a bush from my yard. It was big and overgrowing into my neighbor's side of the fence. Once I did the work to cut the branches down, I came out the next morning to pick them up to see that once disconnected from the root of the tree, their source of growth and nourishment, they had already started to wither away. It reminded me how life works in the same way. When we are not attached to God who is the root for our lives, as branches without the root, we will wither away and die.

A lot of our experiences are cultivated from the choices we make when we do not allow God to be our forefront. Sin does not come without consequences. I have backslid so many times in life, thinking my way was better. But because of His grace and mercy, even through our mistakes, He corrects us and places us back on the right path if that is what we choose.

Jesus was not birthed in ideal circumstances. Instead of the comfort of the Inn to which Mary and Joseph traveled many miles that ultimately had no room for them, Jesus was born in a barn. But he was made King. Being in the wrong place you can miss out on your blessings and you may never suspect where the right place might be, so do not dwell on what you feel you may have lost. At times we can be the biggest obstacle to our own destiny. The first time I flew in an airplane I went to Florida. Towards the end of the flight, before landing, the pilot had to hold back and spin in circles while waiting for a storm to clear before we could proceed. Sometimes God also holds us in limbo to keep us from entering the storm that we do not ourselves see. Other times, we prevent ourselves from moving forward to that wonderful land of palm trees because we are choosing to stay stuck too long in what we know is not deemed for us. Choosing to stay stuck in what was not intended for you and making a choice without God, allows the enemy access to work through the wrong intentions of your heart. For example, you are sure of your stance in a certain situation, but someone is telling you, "I know you want better, I cannot give that to you, but let me continue to waste your time." It is as foolish as it sounds. To be brutally honest, I think some people are for the streets. Not because they must be, but there is the choice to be because there is no desire to work towards anything past what they already know. Some choose not to invest in the work it takes to achieve change. What will you choose?

We are not held hostage or walled off from the kingdom. We are free to choose. God gives us a choice. Therefore, be excited when that person walks away or no longer fits into the long-term goals of your life. Be glad that job you knew you were qualified for did not accept you. Have joy when there are unexpected delays in your plans. Our blessings can be held up on purpose because they are waiting for the traffic, the noise, the accidents, the disruptions to clear. That is God letting you know He is protecting you and He has something and someone else better in store. Remember, He sees the outcomes we do not see. Do not stand at the door that has closed, or in some cases has been shut in your face. Continue walking even when you do not understand.

When I was with my ex-husband, I had tried to see what I could do to buy a home. Year after year, I found myself with a "good job," but I did not necessarily like what I was doing so I was always trying to build up from the job I was leaving. Although the jobs taught me how to be responsible as far as showing up and doing the duties expected of me that I was paid for, these jobs were never enough to get a mortgage loan application in process. The jobs did not pay enough, my credit was not good enough, or my debt to income was too high—it was always something. When certain aspects of life aren't working out for you anymore and you have exhausted all that you can do, it is usually a tell-tale sign that God is ready to do something new in your life.

Before I started working as a bus operator, I was at a job that did not believe in pay increases and undermined my talents and abilities. I was miserable and it was dreadful to wake up and know I was going to work there. When I went through the motions and was hired with the bus company, I struggled with reading maps as I had no sense of direction and became discombobulated at every turn. When it came to a driving exam for the commercial license, I just knew that I quit my job for nothing. For almost two weeks the instructors worked with us on parking and what we would need to pass the road test. When attempting to park even with the cones laid out and the instructor telling me every day how I should steer, once

I saw the triangles in the cones, I was just unable to navigate correctly. I was discouraged and went home after training every day and started to prepare to start the job search all over. The day before the test as I was attempting to park the bus, suddenly, I saw the triangles in the cones and parked the bus perfectly. There were thirteen trainees in the class and only two of us passed the test on the first try. I had never driven anything bigger than a van, not even a U-Haul truck. I studied day and night for the written test to learn all the parts I never knew existed on a vehicle, let alone a bus. Can you tell me that God isn't real?

On the Thanksgiving before the year I bought my home, I needed help with food to be able to make a Thanksgiving dinner for my children, because although I had a new job, funds were limited. I couldn't even imagine that a year and a half later God would position me to be a homeowner. You always get tested the most when you are about to progress to the next level. Two and a half years after I removed myself from my marriage, God placed me in a position with the right job, the right credit at the right time to buy my first property, a three bedroom- two-bathroom townhome that was 2,000 sq ft. It was the first place out of several my family called "home" that really felt like "home" to me. The loan application process was seamless and even though the townhome came with some issues that the sellers knowingly and unknowingly left me with, the home was more than I imagined in buying my first home. God provided me with the ability to newly furnish my home when I moved in. However, the most moving moment for me was when I was able to buy myself my first bedroom set, which included a king size bed because it brought me back to when I was a little girl, and I was not able to have a bed to sleep in comfortably. That was a test that turned into a testimony for me because when I wanted to be a homeowner, I did not see how I would be—between different jobs, or my car getting repossessed because of financial difficulties. It was not meant for me to be a homeowner outside of God's timing because I did not see that my ex-husband was not going to the level God wanted to bring me to. If anyone is in the business to upgrade you, it is God.

There are a lot of times where we hold onto jobs and people with a death grip that will keep us from elevating to the next level in life. When I wanted to buy a home, I was not as financially aware or responsible as I needed to be, and it was hard for me to save a penny. I did not even have a workable budget. If I went to the store and had $5.00 and the total was $3.50, I felt in that case I should spend the whole $5.00, that it did not make sense to save $1.50. With that mentality, I would have ended up in foreclosure fast. God did not give me something that He knew I was not ready to handle. I was able to go from not having a savings cushion and not getting approved for any credit for emergencies to having a means to pay for the unexpected and too much credit available to me. Preapprovals for everything and anything were offered out the woodwork. When my divorce was finalized, it had been exactly four years before that I had exited from the marriage. For a few years prior, it was hard for me to get some jobs because I had a criminal record. I had to go to court on my birthday for my criminal expungement. The day my new social security card came in the mail after six months of waiting and having to resend the paperwork, I had what I needed to officially change my name and because it was on my son's fifth birthday as well, I felt it was a rebirth for me on that day I'd brought life into the world. God is so intentional. Trust God. Trust the process. God loves you.

There comes a time where you realize what you are pouring your energy into is costing you more than it can be worth. Once I had a GMC Arcadia and although I had paid cash for this vehicle and had no car note just weeks after buying it, the transmission went out. I thought to myself, *No big deal, I will just get it fixed* because it was better than a car note. After that there were more mechanical issues, one after another. I just kept pouring money into this vehicle when one day I finally said it was not worth it because I was pouring so much money into the truck, the expenses outweighed the benefits. I was also trying to hold off until I felt that God put me into a position where I could factor in another bill every month. Not even a month later, after getting into a newer SUV, the Acadia conked out completely. We can be in situations like I was with this vehicle, giving so much of ourselves and the returns are not worth it. When are you going to decide to trade in the old for the new and refreshing? What will it take for you to take your hand off the steering wheel and let Jesus take the wheel? I had a car note but I was a lot more stress free knowing that I had a newer vehicle that was not at any given second ready to conk out on me in the middle of the highway.

I would think that most of us always look to get big signs from God. For myself, I wanted Him to come down from heaven and tell me exactly what I needed to do and where I needed to go. That was the only way that I would feel certain about anything happening in my life. One night I was driving and a billboard off the highway caught my eye. All it said was, "Jesus, I trust you." That was confirmation for what I was lacking. I had prayed about asking him what I should do, and he told me. I could feel God's presence in that moment. Emotionally I was overwhelmed because there were no doubts God was speaking to me. I could feel Him smiling at me. Sometimes the smallest messages of confirmation come to us like gifts. Too often, we overlook them.

As the hours turned into days, and the days turned into weeks, I was still grieving and had my moments of weakness. Grief is an emotion that is not always associated with the passing of a person. It is the emotional journey you begin when something is taken away and places you into deep sorrow. I was in grief because the things I once knew, even though not working in my favor, caused me to feel sorrow. It was the dying of the people, things, and positions that I once knew that were gone. Too many times, seeking closure, I stayed stuck even longer in situations and with people. One moment I would feel I got it; then I would feel that I did not get it at all. That keeps you stuck. Your own indecisiveness will be a hinderance in moving forward looking for a closure with a person, thing, feeling, emotion, situation, or when the only thing necessary for you to do is just shut the door and know that God has better for you. There were many moments when I felt lonely, then I could literally feel God filling that space of loneliness. I was feeling stagnate and broken and I heard the spirit clearly saying to me, *I can't move you forward until you let go of this relationship. I can't move you forward until you turn everything over to me that you are dealing with. I can't move until you move. Everything is there for you if you would just let go of your ways and thoughts that do not glorify the name of The Lord.*

Something transformed in me, something uninitiated by my own will and power, where for the first time, I became comfortable in my loneliness. The feelings I had no longer overpowered the desire and pursuit for a life and relationship that honored God with my body, mind, and soul. I could then accept that it was better to be alone than to be somewhere God does not have his hand, or in relationships that did not have any potential to grow. I knew I was someone's future wife and I wanted to conduct myself as such. I knew I was the daughter of a King and I wanted to walk as such, regardless of what the container of my past held and what others thought I would and would not be. Among these strings of hopeful emotions, life was different. These were emotions of finally releasing what held me captive for so much of my life. They were cries of faith, hope, letting go, and trusting in God where I *knew* everything would work out according to his plan and lead me to a place of healing and peace where my path would be straight. It was a sense of freedom and new beginnings, like the sun bursting out of the clouds after the sky delivered days of endless rains.

I had to learn to humble myself. When someone did not pay their bus fare it did not make me any better to intentionally downplay a situation where I could get a discount on something. Just because I was not in the streets stumbling drunk did not make it any less sinful to go out and get drunk at the club. Sin is sin. Romans 3:23 (NLT) states, "For everyone has sinned; we all fall short of God's glorious standard."

There is no doubt change can be hard. But at the end of the day, we are healing, and we are still human, that is where the Grace of God comes in and works supernaturally. When you find yourself going in circles, it is because you have not met the requirements to pass the test to release you from that circle. Everything always starts in the mind before it trickles into any part of your life. As I was getting to know myself better, I recognized more of my triggers to go back to what I used to know. It is not only necessary to occupy your mind with the things above but also to preoccupy your mind. When I was distancing myself from the things and people I wanted to be set apart from, I came to the realization of my own role in faltering because I did not think beforehand, even on things that seemed simple like getting off work or having my days off and what I would do with my time. That became important for me to think about, so that my mind would not automatically channel to doing what I used to do before. I had to change the way I thought about my next moves. There is a need to become more *intentional* in your thoughts because it affects the way that you choose to move. I had to retrain my thought process to think about what I needed or could be doing so I wasn't "weak or bored," or slipping back into positions I knew that I did not want to be in. Even if it was something as simple as going home and deciding what I was going to eat, what tv show I wanted to watch, or maybe even folding those clothes that have been shuffled through and have been in a laundry basket since last week. Second Thessalonians Chapter 3 warns us about idleness. It may seem difficult where you are now, but God has brought you too far to leave and let up on you at this point.

Imagine being in the middle of a brick tunnel. Both entries are blocked and there seems to be no route of escape. Then before you know it, the sides of the tunnel around you come tumbling down providing a way out. That is how God works. He makes a way when there seems to be no way. Take a moment to reflect and write down situations that have occurred in your life when you have seen no way out and God made a way. We get so wrapped up in where we are at the current moment that we forget to reflect on what God has already done for us and we pass over the small victories we have already experienced. During the times when we feel we are surrounded by trouble, doubt, emptiness, hopelessness, helplessness, it is important to reflect on the many ways God has come through for us. Seek freedom from areas of your life and your past hurts that can come with challenges and roller coaster emotions, because everything is possible with the strength of God. I will not sugarcoat it for you because there will be days where it is rough, but it is necessary for you to get up and say, *I am Worthy! I am God's child! I will not be forsaken! I will not be defeated! Satan get behind me! I rebuke you back to the hell you came from!*

There was no one there to tell me, "You got this girl!" But I am telling you, *You Got This!* I had days when I felt I did not do much with my day because I did not feel up to it. On those days, I felt secure in knowing I did my best and that was as much as I could do. If I could only account for it being yet another day where I was able not to resist succumbing to my emotions and the hungers of my flesh, and was able to withstand the temptation to fall back into the self-destructive mindset I previously had, that was an accomplishment. I was a moving box filled with breakables. Placing and handling myself the wrong way could subject me to breaking again. You must become aware of the triggers that have previously led you to regress. Starve what you want to die and feed what you want to grow. Give yourself permission to handle your package with delicacy for there is no race and rush. It can be heavy to think so far ahead when going through a major life transition that is uncomfortable, because change will cause you to be uncomfortable as you grow from what you have previously known. It is ok to take it one day at a time. If you feel good today, do not worry about the next day because that day has its own worries. *Embrace today*. God has given you the grace you need for the day. Each day I could literally feel myself rising a bit more out of the fire and I began to feel cool air come upon me. When you are putting a band-aid over a wound that requires surgery and not utilizing the best doctor you have readily available to you, it will be impossible to fully recover from anything until that revelation has transpired.

I would watch this show on the HGTV network called, "Love It or List It." People would come on the show to have their homes renovated but be given a choice to buy another home that was suitable for their new needs and advanced desires for a home if their current home did not meet their renovation standards. It reminded me how God is in the business of renovations and restorations and after you've been restored, you turn out better than you ever imagined. no matter where you came from, or in this analogy, no matter which home the family chose.

Chapter 10—Setting The Pace

Nowadays it is so easy for us to become offended when someone calls us out on our stuff or when we feel that people have wasted our time. I once had a supervisor tell me that I would put a man above my children because my desire for a husband was so strong. After scolding her, I thought it is always easier to critique and judge when you are not standing where someone else is in their journey, and you already have your husband. She also told me that change would not happen in my life until I was truly ready to change. This same supervisor was the energy The Lord used to push me forward in the process of buying a home for which I would never have known that I would qualify until I went through the process of submitting my information. Later that same evening after my supervisor told this to me, I submitted my application for a mortgage loan. Difficult people do come into our lives for a reason.

Neither Robert nor my ex-husband were the right men for me but while trying to do things my way, both long-term relationships were catalysts to get me where God me to be, because these men pushed me to the point of wanting to uncover the secrets within me, what I was hiding from, and those discoveries led me to a journey of healing and to fully dedicate my life to Jesus. The marriage I thought would be my one and only was used as an example of what marriage was not in God's covenant. I spent fifteen years in two relationships with two people who were not suited for me. I could have circled around several different men to learn the same lesson, but I settled for two who gave me a run for my money as if I had been with several. I think that it is important to note when we have been in a relationship with someone several years and come out of it feeling like our youth and our time was wasted, that time is not to be dwelled upon, only celebrate that you did not stay stuck even longer. It is all for preparation. God will use certain situations and/or people that you may feel are against you to fulfill his message to you and that message may break you completely down so that you can come forward to Him, the one that will supply all of what you need. God, the Father of our Lord Jesus Christ may beckon you to a place where you no longer want to pacify your needs and desires but to experience life, healing, a sense of wholeness, purpose, and peace. It is important to weather the storms in our lives because the rain is a necessity. The rain allows for new growth. Don't plants need water to blossom? If there is no water, the plant will just wither away—sometimes slowly, other times at a rapid speed. Also plants do not always grow in the light. Sometimes we are hidden in the dark so that we can grow. It can take nothing but thirty seconds to break you down, but it is costly to be rebuilt.

In my house as a child, I was isolated; I could never invite company over. I was barely allowed to go outside. When neighborhood kids would knock on the door to inquire if I could play outside, they were turned away or lied to, told that I was not home. Enduring this treatment, I became accustomed to having no friends or craving social interaction. Of course, I never suspected that this was what I would need twenty years down the line when God needed to isolate me. However, I intentionally began to seek isolation when I worked out of one bus garage and then transferred to another because I wanted to be free of distractions. I got used to isolation and it was familiar. I wanted to be completely focused on walking in my purpose.

Although I did interact with Robert again after the evening I cried out to Jesus for deliverance. Unannounced, Robert showed up at my home to offer an apology that was no longer needed or authentically given, and I wasn't tempted to go back to how we previously were. By then, peace had already settled my spirit so that there was no more debate over having him in my life. It may seem as if I have given my relationship with Robert a lot of "glorification" because I have discussed in detail my situation with him. The truth of the matter is—it isn't so much about Robert. It's much, much, much bigger.

We all have that one life encounter which is our "end all." It may be for someone else who had been addicted to drugs all their life and then one day they overdose to a point where it almost costs them their life. It's not until then that they are able to recover from drug addiction. For another person, it may be doing something illegal which lands them in jail for the first time, or a long sentence after the seventeenth time, where it is decided they never want to see inside of a jail cell again. The turning point for others may be something as simple and beautiful as bringing life into the world for the first time. The bigger picture is something transpiring that reaches so deeply into your soul, there is no choice but to respond with an authentic need for God.

Robert was that "end of the rope" for me. My "Come-to-Jesus" moment. Sometimes deliverance does not look, feel, or take place how we think it should. I imagined being delivered and not speaking to or seeing Robert again. Despite the fact I did talk to him a few more times after the cussing-me-out incident, and the unannounced house visit, it did not make me feel any less delivered. I did not have the urge to fornicate with him, to go out and party with him and pick up where we left off as I had done many times before. I stopped drinking so I could have a clear mind and did not want the effects of alcohol to disrupt my open and transparent spirit. I did not have that "feel good" juice that makes everything seem okay for the moment when it is indeed *not*. I came to the realization that at times deliverance does not have anything to do with the person we are praying to be delivered from. Most times, it is our own ways and paths that God is working to deliver us from. I could have met another "Robert" or another "ex-husband" and be sucked back into the same cycles I prayed to be out of, but if your inner core does not change, it does not matter if the person is different or not. Deliverance from my negative characteristics dissolved my need for sex. I only desired to make love to the husband whom God presented and approved of. God delivered me from loneliness and that was something with which I had struggled deeply—the idea that I could not feel complete until I had a partner. I was also delivered from seeking validation from others, from the pain I endured with family relationships to so-called friends and romantic relationships. Deliverance is a choice that must be made every day. What good is getting delivered from the person or things you are wanting to leave behind if nothing changes within? You'll just end up with the same character wearing a different face. You're worried about how the finished project is going to look when you don't even have the materials to start the building.

God does allow events to happen to us to build our trust and love in Him—our character, our strength—yet we are still shielded from a lot that could have happened. His grace always covers us, even when we are in sin. He chooses us not because of anything we do or did not do. He delivers us time, time, time and time again because He loves us. I love the bible verse Romans 8:35. "Who shall ever separate us from Christ's love? Shall suffering and affliction and tribulation? Or calamity and distress? Or persecution or hunger or destitution or peril or sword?" There is nothing that can separate us from the love of God.

I felt I had cried so many tears. Where were my tears from? From my mother leaving me to be swallowed up with nothing but misfortune and unforgiveness? From my marriage not working out? From my children no longer being raised in a two-parent home? From a man not loving me correctly? From being taken for granted by someone I knew could not fit the shoe for the job? Someone who I did not really want to be with? From the lack of confirmation sent to validate what I felt? From Family and friends no longer around because it was not meant for them to enter the next level in my journey?

You might ask when will the pain be enough to bring this process to an end? When things you have prayed for begin to manifest and this person or these things you felt you loved so much and could not let go of won't even be a thought again. When I would go around "family," I could not understand why I felt uneasy, out of place, and that I didn't belong. When I kept retreating to the cycle of entertaining certain places, relationships and so-called friendships, my peace was disrupted. Have you ever looked at the definition of peace in the Merriam-Webster dictionary? It represents a quiet and calm state of mind. You need to have a craving for peace for yourself despite what you have been through, what someone has done to you, or what they didn't do for you. Peace is priceless. Stop ignoring the feeling you have in your heart when the Holy Spirit is blessing it with revelations. The Holy Spirit gives us discernment about people and/or situations yet we still choose to ignore them. How long will you ignore the Holy Spirit? How broken do you need to be to realize that particular relationship is not what Jesus intended for you? How long will you keep holding on to what others have done against you? How long will it take for you to stop getting in your own way and begin the transition God wants to take you through because He is giving you signs about what needs to be done. He does not want you to live alone and without Him.

Once I came to the realization that God did not remove anything from my life that He thought I would need, it became easier to accept the things that I fought against. I chose not to sit in my weaknesses and disappointments. I was writing this book while

I was going through some of these passages as well as healing and the many tears that fell onto these pages came from the darkest time in my life. Some days it took everything in me to even get out of bed, to go to work, even to take care of my children. Talk about being broken— there were days I wanted to die because the pain was so unbearable as I was reliving what I felt and had been through. It hurt even more that I selfishly thought only of myself and leaving my children with the trauma of their mother taking her own life. I finally embraced the fact there was no divine love at the core of the things I loved. Knowing the place I was in was not the place God desired for me to be helped me to push forward no matter what—to see these ties to the people of my past and the stronghold they'd had on my destiny completely dissolve with all my unresolved trauma. The love of God that I knew He had for me made it easier to accept my choice to fight and persevere no matter what I was up against, to pass the tests I was repeatedly presented with because I did not receive the message. I wanted someone who desired me as I much as I desired him. As much as God desired me and I desired God. The point to learn is to seek relationships with others who complete your purpose not just you as a person. You need to be complete yourself, as an individual, before you can add in another person. I had to learn that no human can fill in the void of incompleteness when you are dealing with past traumas and relationships and identity issues. It is not possible to say that you are a faithful player if you only show up for half of the season. Check that the actions align with the thoughts and words.

It is deep when you can say I trust God to bring into my life a spouse, but I am still entertaining less than what I want and what I deserve. Can you honestly say you have put God first as the source for all your heart, life, and well-being? I continuously circled longer than I wanted but I realized that was necessary in the end to really get the big picture. When you find you are repeatedly circling around the same type of issues, that is a deep indication you have not tried God wholeheartedly. It is time to settle the dust. It is time to release your whole life to Him. He is giving you the layout to build something that will not falter and fail but is to be built on a solid foundation.

When we are alone and broken and broken down, which I was, we are pressured to become the jewels that God has designed for us to be. Isolation can mean elevation. It gets easy to feel left out. It hurts to think what you desire will not come but hold on! Waiting does not always mean no or never! While I was transitioning my life to God there were people who counted me out, who saw me as no more or less than what I was at that time. This will happen. My mother was the first of many who saw me as no more than this rebellious teenager who would never amount to anything. This is a tactic of the devil to discourage you, to fill your spirit with uncertainty, so that maybe you will not reach for "better," not knowing all the while God has a calling for you. I was there and some of the best things to have ever happened to me happened then. The day I chose to surrender everything in my life past and present to God, a light was revealed to me I had never experienced before. It wasn't a physical feeling, more so spiritual, and emotional, transitioning from anything I had previously known; all of the past being stripped away. The heaviness that was always with me in my heart, subsided. I began to crave to be closer to God in reading the Bible, praying and spending time with Him, not just because I was in trouble or wanted to make a request for something. I was no longer feeling angry for no apparent reason or being triggered from my past in a negative reaction. I felt compassion for my enemies. My purpose became clear to me, after job shuffling for many years. I felt peace within the problems I encountered and genuine forgiveness for those I felt hurt me because I realized I could not fully understand what the grace of God meant without them. It was like a lightning bolt struck to my entire being that said, "you have a mission and you have work to do." It was the spirit of God that He was truly there for me, and He was all I needed.

In most cases, people who are toxic for you are not happy with some part(s) of themselves. Remember the saying, "misery loves company." It is difficult to bring themselves up, so it is easier for them to tear down other people. Usually there is no productive progression in their lives and since you have met them, nothing has elevated them, therefore you can basically predict their every move, thought, and/or reaction to a situation. If you keep finding yourself "setback" or your spirit feels disturbed and uneasy every time you dabble with this person, it is time to take control and slam the door shut so you can truly move on with the Lord and the will he has for you. Stop answering their calls, stop responding to the texts. I would suggest changing your number if possible or blocking them. Stop making excuses for them. Stop checking their social media profiles to see what they are up to. It is no longer any of your concern. Stop allowing them to infiltrate your being keeping you stuck!

I even experienced this with the family I was born into. I wanted the idea of having an extended family, but as I have mentioned, I had always felt out of place being around them. I was close to a cousin named Tara, my aunt Linda's daughter, who was like the sister I did not have. We did everything together and would talk on the phone multiple times a day for hours at a time. There was a time we could have died together when we were involved in a car accident. After leaving a bar we were both very intoxicated, and we were a block from her house and she flipped over the truck we were driving attempting to avoid a construction cone she'd seen last minute on a rainy night. When I had Michael, she stayed in the hospital room with me until my son and I were released from the hospital which was a week because as mentioned before my son was in the NICU and an emergency cesarean birth. There were a few incidents over the years that occurred that made me question her loyalty, but I overlooked them.

For instance, even when I was on welfare, I might suggest we go to McDonald's to get burgers and shakes on a summer day too hot to cook. She would not have any money and although my funds were limited, I would pay for hers too. One day she did have some money and we ordered food thru the drive through and what I ordered came up to $5.00. Instead of her paying for the total bill as I had done for her many times before, she extended her hand saying she needed my portion. In this same time frame, she was dating a man in a half-way house after he was released from prison, and never hesitated to give him money or buy him food and other items. So indeed, I was very taken aback. In the same way, I was taken aback when she seen nothing wrong with how her mom treated Michael and I when for the short time we stayed at their home. She simply stated, "My mom don't want nobody staying at her house. This isn't my house. I can't do anything about it." It wasn't that she was right in a sense, it was the nonchalant disdain in her attitude as she said it to me. Whenever she had an issue with someone, she would call me to do a three-way call with her to have her back, yet when I was battling Sam's family by myself and asked Tara to go to bat for me on social media, she gave a million excuses of why she didn't want to. Saying, "that don't have anything to do with me." She suggested to just leave it alone and ignore it. Yet I never questioned her motives and choices when I went to war for her, without a second thought on three-way calls. I could have also said, "that has nothing to do with me, just let it go," although at the end of the day going back and forth with anyone is just childlike and not worth it. Then one day her brother, (who was also my cousin) made a sexual advance towards me while we were at her home. We were all outside, hanging out on the sidewalk in front of Tara's house with a few other people since the duplex she was staying at did not have air conditioning. While no one was looking her brother came up behind me and smacked my butt. Just a few weeks before at a birthday party he also made an inappropriate comment saying, "You know us being cousins doesn't have to mean anything." Mind you this was my first cousin, his mom Linda and my mom are sisters. The next day when I broke down and told Tara about it, there was dead silence on the other end of the line. She then told me, "I don't know what happened because I was busy talking, I didn't see it." Hurt and shock traveled through my body at that moment and tears began to fill my brown eyes. I knew I could never deal with her again. I knew at that moment who her loyalty was truly with and that was the last straw for me in dealing with the family I was born into. I completely let them all go.

There had been other allegations in the family about uncles and other male cousins making sexual advances to other female family members and now I couldn't help but to think there was some level of truth to them. I would later realize and accept they were not meant to stay where God intended to take me. The feeling of uneasiness and being out of place when I was around them eventually dissipated. I have known of a lot of situations where people get wrapped up with family and blood ties are all that you have in common. Some people are in your life for you to simply to get over. There is no requirement to deal with blood family members regardless of how you are treated or feel. Family can keep you stuck too! You cannot experience the full and abundant blessings God has for you if you keep holding onto what he has already removed from your life. It's not to say you will not receive any blessings, but you hold yourself hostage from receiving the overflow.

As I was transitioning into my healing journey, I reached out to my sisters in an attempt to make amends and although we were separated from each other by the hands of our mother, I felt I wanted to attempt to salvage what we had lost over so many years and form a sisterly bond. There was a concert in the state of Rhode Island where they lived, with artists that I enjoyed listening to and I was willing to fly out and foot the expenses for us to go as well as talk and come to an understanding with each other, rehash the past a final time and bury it. I thought we could face what we went through as a family together so we could build a relationship and bond. Although my intentions were pure, I prayed and asked God for guidance. The trip did not occur because my spirit was uneasy. You can't explain your journey and where you are headed to those whose hearts are not open or meant to receive and understand. I put a lot of time into this throughout my life and my efforts went nowhere. It was like talking to a wall. My sisters still held onto more of the past than I did, especially with the relationship I had with our mother and when the trip did not materialize, in my spirit I knew that was God saying to me, *I delivered you from that* and He was not taking me back to rehash the non-existent, short-lived relationship with our mom, and the person I no longer was. I had done too much work within to go back, and God set up the encounter so that I would not go back. My mother may never admit it, but she was the parental figure that played a major role in ensuring my siblings and I would not be able to grow up together and establish a bond. As the saying goes: "Hurt people hurt people."

Another person's denial and betrayal can be the most awesome blessing because it weeds out the counterfeit. I was angry for years about the situation with my mother and now I was authentically able to rejoice that God did not leave me stuck there. He loves us enough to pull us out and make us better while doing it, resulting in a gratitude that I could experience after coming from a dark place. We do not need anyone to save us, but God, and he is so wonderful and magnificent He will even catch us when we fall.

Do not continue to get sucked back into what you were inspired to walk away from because you are afraid of feelings that are uncomfortable or what society deems as "normal." Those emotions and feelings need to be felt. Depression is real. Heartache is real. Feeling like you cannot go on another day, let alone another second, is real. *God is Real!* Your heart and your mind-frame need transformation to grow and gain a different perspective. Growth pains will accompany your transformation. Take your emotions out of the situation and take a glance back with a rational mindset. Look at the bigger picture of your life. Have you always stayed stuck in any one situation? Think back to the situations you saw yourself dealing with and notice how God worked it out in your favor, whether it was the outcome you were expecting and prayed for—or not.

Which sounds better for you, the pain from the growth, or the pain from being stuck in something or with someone that is truly not for you? It's all a matter of perspective. Sometimes we are too close to our problem to see it, so a necessary step is to back away to analyze the situation from the outside. Embrace the time in transition and peel back the layers to get to know yourself. You may ask how do I go about doing that? First by spending time with God. Open your Bible and talk with Him. God is a good listener in a no judgement zone. You talk to Him by digging into past traumas and what you took away from them, both the good and the bad. Be thankful at all times for what seems insignificant at the moment as there are many blessings even in our storms, such as the breath in your body, or another day to push forward toward your goals. Learn what moves you. I'll say it again: *Distance yourself from relationships that no longer serve where you are in life.* Journaling is a good outlet for reflection, even if it is just regarding how your day went. When you look it over later sometimes you realize something you weren't aware of at the moment you were writing. Read. Listen to music that is joyful and uplifting. Take trips by yourself to places around town you have never been and have always wanted to go. Notice the little things that make you smile.

God did not intend for you to surround yourself with the ones who do not love you and appreciate you, those who draw you far from him—the ones who will bring you down a path not ordained for your life. Think of yourself investing in a house but the people you have allowed to stay there are trashing it and it is causing your investment to lose value. Are you going to protect your investment or keep letting your home be destroyed? Think of yourself, your life as that home. *You* are the investment. You have a duty to value yourself and to remove anyone or anything that is not adding to your life but is depreciating your value.

I felt guilty for a long time that I struggled so much to feel a temperament of forgiveness, mercy, and love towards the ones who had hurt me. I wanted to show them the same grace that God had continually shown me when I chose time and time again to walk in darkness. The power of forgiveness is not to be underestimated. In your healing it is a requirement to release unforgiveness for yourself as well as others. I knew that forgiving at a level I could not understand was possible because God had helped me get there before. I needed to be able to walk away from a situation regardless of any apology rendered to me, despite the other person recognizing, admitting, or initiating to correct their faults.

Slowly, for my own mother, feelings of anger, pain, and unforgiveness began to be replaced with empathy, forgiveness, and peace. Because the same little girl I was, the one who left in a state void of love, unprotected, thrown out alone to fend for herself, that was the same little girl my mother had to be. She gave to me what she only knew to give as a parent. But I wanted to let my resentment go for the sake of my intimate spiritual relationship with God. I knew that I could not come full circle if I had the feelings of bitterness and unforgiveness buried in my heart. I wanted to let go and move on for my mental and emotional stability, for the sake of my relationship with my own children, for the sake of my own life. *Forgiveness is not for the person who has hurt you but for yourself to be free and live in your spirit peacefully.* Forgiveness releases you from bondage to the ill feelings that can linger when you are clutching onto what someone has done to you. *Choose to forgive. Choose to be free.*

People will change when and if they are ready to change. That process cannot, I repeat, *cannot* be forced, no matter the ultimatums, the fuss, and repeated arguments. Not if you want it to be genuine. When it is real, it cannot and will not be forced under any circumstance. If you are talking with someone and they are responding by speaking another language which you do not understand, are you going to continue to sit there and utter noises at them? You cannot be on the same page because you are speaking two different languages, therefore your need is not being met. How long will you make a useless effort before giving up? Being involved with the wrong person(s) can lead to someone stealing your purpose, and to you relinquishing your dreams, and undermining your honest, and sincere alignment with God. You are not meant to prove your worth. Yes, there is a difference of showing your good qualities and what you can bring to the table, but you should not be acting in the role of a sale persons pitching your product. The right people will be just as equally pushing to prove themselves to you. Your worth must be seen and should never have you in a position to beg for it to be recognized. You do not look for others to validate your value. You are validated by God. You validate and value yourself. Only you can choose to hold yourself to the highest standards, and that is reflected by the choices you make, and the choices that are not so good that you continue to make and do not attempt to correct. Whether it's with family, friends, or a partner, do not place yourself in the company of those who make you feel you are unworthy. If they make you feel like what you are asking of them is too much, leave them at their own level.

There is such a thing as reasonable expectations. It is reasonable to expect to be respected. It is reasonable to expect your friend to be there for you when you are in need. It is reasonable to share expenses with a mate and to ask someone to get a job if necessary. It is reasonable to ask for romance and occasional date nights. It is reasonable to want to be involved with someone who has a relationship with God at their core. It is reasonable to expect someone to be faithful to you. It is reasonable to be able to have trust in a relationship. Don't allow anyone to devalue and manipulate you at your own expense, while they to continue to play off your emotions and rob you of a better future by playing the victim. They are just not the one capable of meeting your needs and that is okay. Everybody is not for everybody. For every season there is something and/or someone. You do not have a duty to force anyone to change because if the need for change is authentic, it will happen organically. It is not worth the effort to try and force someone to share your values and goals when in the end, you will only carry away the feeling of disappointment towards the person and yourself, when you have not stood firm on your worth, values, beliefs. When the signs and symptoms are open to you, observe and take action.

I had to learn to be content wherever God led me. To embrace the wisdom given to me, even when I did not hear His voice to give me directions or the next instructions, I knew that did not always mean I was getting it wrong. The teacher does not always speak during a test. I struggled with being "out of place" for a long time and felt that somewhere I was left behind, not realizing where I was—was where God wanted me, even if I did not understand what was going on around and within me, that the blocks would be used as steppingstones. Psalms 23:1 (NIV) says, "The Lord is my Shepard, I lack nothing. He makes me lie down in green pastures, He leads me besides quiet waters, He refreshes my soul. He guides me along the right paths for His name's sake. Even though I walk through the darkest valley, I will fear no evil, for You are with me; your rod and your staff, they comfort me." That Bible verse is so soothing to the soul to again remind you that God is with you always.

Chapter 11—All Glory Be To God

Unshakable faith. Faith is closing your eyes and putting your hands over your eyes. Even with the darkness, you are confident that you are going into a surprise you cannot see, but you know you are walking into something good, although it has not been revealed to you yet. Faith is trusting when you have no proof. You do not have a tracking number for when God is going to show up or an ETA, but you know that He is there and no matter what it looks like, what you are praying and seeking for wholeheartedly is on the way. Faith is trusting God when you believe what you are facing is not bigger than Him. Stop putting limits on what God can do. He has brought you too far to leave you. If he brought you out of illness, poverty, addiction, abuse, domestic violence, homelessness, sadness, depression, anxiety, the hands of the justice system, why are you choosing to be stuck and doubting that God will deliver you from this very thing you are dealing with at this moment? God's timing is not our timing, but He is always an on-time God.

Eventually you will get tired of your self-destructive thoughts, and behaviors that led you into situations and relationships that in the end held some level of regret. Not trusting God and wholeheartedly surrendering myself was the step I had continuously missed when attempting to take the struggle upon myself to fix what I thought and knew needed fixing. Earlier in my life I had lacked faith in God's plans and will, which I now know exceeds anything I could ever do on my own in a lifetime. Once I surrendered to allowing God to have His way with my life, I came to the realization that being broken down to my very core after so many years was all for a purpose. I just did not know what the purpose was. The regrets faded and were cultivated into priceless life lessons that brought me back to where God wanted me to be. I knew my journey, my heartbreak, disappointments, inadequacies, and tests that had become testimonies, were not in vain.

Your pain is not in vain. However, you cannot just trust God when the weather conditions are clear. You need to trust Him when the conditions are dry or icy, rainy, fiercely windy with thunderstorms, or when it is so foggy you can't see a thing in the distance. You need to trust Him *AT ALL TIMES!* We are still human at the end of the day and God knows this. It is okay to pass through feelings of resentment, hopelessness, anger, hurt, disappointment, weariness, overwhelm, rejection and loneliness. I have felt all of these emotions. And at times—I felt them all at one time! The goal is not to succumb to those feelings and get stuck in them. Instead, let them pass through you. What solution and outcome does it render you to sit in these emotions besides allowing the devil to come and make your situation his playground?

The memory that sticks out in my mind from a young age, a situation where I had the ability to adapt and overcome despite what I was faced with—was the rejection I encountered in fourth grade when I tried out for the school choir. I was always a bit shy, but I mustered up enough courage to audition. The day of the audition I was both excited and nervous. The next day the list went up by the music room door with the names of the children who had made it. My name was not on that list. I scrolled up and down the list again. Nope, my name was not there. Rejection hit me like a ton of bricks. I felt in that moment as inadequate as I had ever felt as a nine-year-old. In that moment I felt I was not even good enough to get into something as simple as a school choir. I had no parental support or friends, so I suffered quietly. When auditions came around the next year, I was faced with the choice to audition again with the heightened fear that it was possible I would fail to make the roster again. I set those feelings to the side and signed my name on the audition board. I went to the audition with courage big enough to move a mountain and made sure I sang loud enough to be heard. Despite the previous year's rejection, I was going full force as if it had never happened. When the list came out, I knew that I had given it everything I had and did my best without fear in my body. Again, I scrolled down the list of students' names. This time my name was on the list. I had made the final cut.

You may feel left behind but it is dire to always trust the process. Something

that happens to you that seems insignificant when you are young can play a major factor in what Jesus knows you will experience and need as an adult. Where you are now is leveling you up for what is yet to come. This rejection I experienced at nine years old set me up for life trials that I would experience when I became much older. I learned that rejection one time does not mean repeated rejection the next time around, and that not trying is worse than being disqualified. I learned to be thankful for what I went through because it was built on what God was bringing me to.

Over time I'd worked a lot of minimum wage jobs that I'd committed to and worked as if I was working for a large professional group, and that built up my endurance and sense of responsibility to arrive at a position with higher pay. My work ethics were groomed so that when the right job with the exact pay I needed fell into my lap, I could afford to buy a home for my children. I knew how not to take that higher pay position for granted. If I had bought the house at the time I had first I wanted, I think I may have been in a house that was set up for foreclosure. I wasn't aware that I was still missing key ingredients to be a responsible homeowner. When I did buy a home, I was not inclined to buy the latest fashions, run up my credit cards, maxing them out as I previously did. I was groomed to know what it was like to budget and live within my means and I have never missed a house payment, even with a past history of paying late rent payments and an unlawful detainer.

God says you are doing too much. Just slow down. Too many times we are busy trying to peak at the next person's test when we are not even taking the same test. It is not always about praying to God to remove the storm but asking for his guidance and strength to weather the storm and reveal His purpose. Get up! Choose to be better not bitter! Healed and not broken! Not a victim but a victor! In this very moment be encouraged, be proud, love yourself, pursue your dreams, forgive, and let God take care of the rest. Our trials and the journeys are far bigger than we can grasp. God has His purpose for you. The trials that are meant to break you came to strengthen you, make you wiser, stronger, yet humbled, and closer to God. Choose not to be a prisoner in life's circumstances. Stop putting limits on what you think God can and will do for you. Don't just focus on the test, focus on the testimony!

There are also the many faces of distraction that satan will use to try to deter you from living in the purpose God wants for you. The face does not necessarily need to be that of a human face but could be the face of drugs, alcohol, sexual indulgence, depression, anxiety, guilt, hurt, the thoughts we think. I was faced with distractions and was consumed by them in a depth that affected my day-to-day life, so concerned to know if God had a spouse for me. I was consumed with what my ex-husband was and was not doing to help me with our children. Robert himself was a distraction emotionally, mentally, and sexually.

What if I have written this book from my heart and soul and it does not reach people the way I intend to reach them? *That thought* is a distraction. How about the distraction and anxiety of being at a job that provides, keeps my head above water, but is not my passion? What if I was stuck being a bus driver forever? It is a choice everyday what noises you allow into your frame of thinking. It is imperative to have a prayer life, continually seeking God's guidance and waiting faithfully on Him. He will give you the answers, guide your path and show you the way. We need to live by the standards of the Lord. Give yourself time to analyze the situation at hand and watch before diving in headfirst. I remember there was this guy at my job who was a vault puller when the buses pulled in to get the day's cash box and replace it with an empty cash box. I thought he was a nice guy but I did not want to rush into giving him my number. I prayed on it and waited. Not much time passed, and it was revealed to me in my spirit that he carried a lot of the same characteristics I had dealt with previously and I knew for certain he was no longer acceptable to me. I noted how he was stuck in his ways and what I had seen was all that I would be getting. The man God has for you will not be "perfect" because it's a fact, none of us are—but that man will be perfect for you when God aligns it His way. That man will love you and have God in the forefront of his life because the love you deserve and how you should be loved can only flow from the love that he himself has for God. As I saw myself going from one relationship to the next, as I grew more into myself and what I had to offer as a woman of Christ, I could see why the men I had chosen and been involved with did not see my qualities and embrace me as I had wanted. I look back and see that God did not hold the highest position in their lives. In every area of your life, it is time to hold yourself to the standard that God sees in you. You are His child, His masterpiece. Put the trash out! When the trashman comes the garbage is taken away and you never think about it again, let alone see it again. Time to take the trash out! There is no more looking in the rearview. It is time to look through the windshield.

It is not about looking how far ahead in the journey you need to go but looking back on how far God has brought you with the grace and mercy that He continuously bestows on your life, which is the only thing you should ever look back on. The further you push forward the more you desire not to go back to the things and people God has carried you away from that do not align with His will and His purpose for your life. The more courage you muster to have to walk through the fire, no matter what it looks like, the more pressure the devil will use to try and tempt you. But you will crave much more to be close to God and feel his truth. *You need the test to have a TESTimony! Your breakdown is your breakthrough!* It is a choice every day either to trust God or to worry. The love of Christ is watching over your life. If there were sacrifices that I needed to make to go through what I went through as a child, even my mis-steps in early motherhood, in order to be a good mother, supportive and loving to my own children, it was worth it. If the dead-end relationships had to fail to make space for the relationships that honor God and that are for me, it was worth it. If my pain, brokenness, sorrows, tests, and tribulations were what I had to go through to be a helper in the next person's healing journey, it was worth it. Your trials are not in vain!

I think back and wonder if my mother knew the same God I knew? Did she read the same Bible I had read? The God I knew was "a father to the fatherless" says Psalms 68:5. The God I knew said He would never leave me or forsake me, that is what is written in Hebrews 13:5. It says that despite my circumstances and the choices I made or did not make, God had me in the palms of His hand and I was designed and destined to win and conquer the storms. The friends I wanted to have that did not accept me, I now know were not meant to be a part of my journey and not having them turned out in my favor. Did my ex-husband's family know I was God's daughter and "no weapon formed against me shall prosper"? (Psalms 54:17) My character was attacked, my faith, my integrity compromised, lied about, mistreated. Did the memo go unreceived to the man who participated in the conception of my first-born son, leaving me young and homeless to raise this child on my own expecting like my own mother—for me to fail and not know that I am the Daughter of a King? Jesus was betrayed by one of his disciples. So why should we think we are exempt from people who will betray us? Like Jesus, that same betrayal was part of the plan to work toward the good in my life. My point is that no matter what anyone has done to you or where you started in life, God has you and he is not finished with you. You can decide today to no longer be a victim but a victor and survivor of your circumstances. You can decide that you will not be broken, but by the grace of our Loving God, you will be healed. Your start does not have to be deemed your finish. Deliverance feels like a tug of war. Change and seeking to be set free from the life of your past can be hard; it can be uncomfortable and seem at times impossible. It is like cleaning out your refrigerator. You are reorganizing, throwing out the stuff you know has been in there past its expiration date, and you discover the food that was old and without nutrition, spoiled food that you did not know was there. But you keep whatever you know is still fruitful and good.

While you are working to become closer to God, satan is trying to discourage you and pull you back. *But you've got this!* You are on the path to being delivered. Do not give up! Finish this race because victory is around the corner and closer than you may feel and know. You need to literally PUSH. *Pray* until something happens. *Pray* until you hear those chains falling. *Pray* until the chains are broken. *Pray* until thinking about those past hurtful experiences does not affect and trigger you in the negative ways it did before. *Pray* until you are free and *pray* to continue to remain free. Anything and everything is possible when your strength comes from God.

My heart's desire is to have you stop in your tracks right now and lay down all your burdens, your sorrows, your worries, your doubts, your unforgiveness, your past traumas, your insecurities, your confusion, your indecisiveness, your fears, leave it all at His feet. Finally, let go of the need to know every detail about how it is going to work out. It's important to let go of the need to feel some type of control and instead appreciate the season God has you in, no matter what it looks like. Blessings, trials and/or neutrality. We are broken to heal. Even after all you have GROWN through, you are still undefeated! You have not been knocked down and out for the count because you have already won. Without the process of stripping you down, there is no way to gloss up!

I hear the devil saying, *Your own family didn't want you*, but I hear God saying, *I am your Father*. I hear the devil saying, *You are washed up and used, no man will want you*, and I hear God saying, *I will wipe you clean*. I hear the devil saying, *You're too broken to come out of this* and I hear God saying, *I will heal you*. I hear the devil saying, *Nobody loves you*, and I hear God saying, *I love you*. I hear the devil saying, *Your talents are not sufficient* and I hear God saying, *I will give you everything and need to use you as a vessel*. God is calling you! How long will you let Jesus stand at the door? When are you going to answer Jesus' call and let Him in to bring you the change and healing you need?

Now the question remains, are you determined to run away from God's purpose or run towards it? This reminds me of the Biblical story of Jonah. Jonah tried to run away from what God instructed him to do and thought it was sweet that he could just get on the ship and leave, not expecting God to place barriers into the mix. Yet and still, it brought Jonah back to where God wanted him to be and what He wanted Jonah to do. You may have realized I have not mentioned any therapy or counseling. It was another determining factor in my journey I contemplated many times. Here is my stance: I am not against counseling or any type of therapy. I advocate for the people who feel they need it to seek professional help. For me however, every time I made an appointment to start therapy sessions something always seemed to transpire. I made an appointment with one therapist and he did not do talk therapy only medication. I set another appointment and after waiting for two months, two weeks before the appointment the clinic called and stated that the therapist I was going to see had decided to retire. I did not feel therapy was a necessity, but it does appear to work for a lot of people who go down that avenue. I had others who said I needed counseling to filter through my mess and focus on what I wanted to work on. What I learned throughout that experience is that counseling and medication is not necessary for everyone. I am not in any way knocking it if that is your preference. If it is helping you or has helped you, I encourage it. However, at times, for some of us, the therapy that is needed is a breakthrough of divine intervention that must come from God. He did it for me and he can and will do it for you. I have broken from ways, things, people I never saw myself being freed of, as well as situations that had a such a strong grip on me, I needed something more than a weekly talk session.

It started with me intentionally seeking God's face, every moment of my day, spending time with God and in his presence, reading his word, listening to music that was uplifting and magnified his name, as well as many YouTube sermons. It is essential to do everything that you do with a purpose. Like cleaning your house. The purpose is to keep your home from welcoming rodents and smelling like garbage. When you date, date with purpose for a goal of marriage and being equally yoked with someone who desires to serve Christ. When you parent your children, be intentional on the purpose to raise healthy wholesome adults.

Today is the day you ask God to forgive you and let God know you are here. Say *I am letting go.* Say *I lay all my burdens at your feet.* Childhood trauma, relationships and situationships, trauma and dysfunction, unforgiveness, fear, worry, feelings of defeat, depression, anxiety, low self-confidence, and low self-esteem, how others have wronged me for the job that I didn't get, for the job I have that is not fulfilling and feeding my soul. I let go of financial stress, and the purpose for my life that I am conflicted about. I let go of sickness, disease, addiction, my role as a parent, loneliness, my ability to have children, rejection, my desire for a kingdom-based marriage and healthy relationships. I let go of not having it all figured out, of feeling I am not good enough or talented enough, and all else that can be laid at the feet of the Lord to take the burden off my shoulders.

My purpose is to let you know with God ALL things will and do get better. I know when it is hard to see past your circumstances because the pressure is so much at the time. God doesn't let you go through anything he knows you will not be able to handle. If God, has you at a certain point in life, he knows you can handle it, he knows the other side of the situation. It is the enemy's trick to discourage you and weaken your spiritual relationship because then you submit yourself to be tossed and turned like a tumbleweed blown in any direction the wind takes you.

By all means please come into this new place of healing for you. God is the doctor who takes care of it all! Your crown did not fall off, it just needed a little adjusting. If you are looking for permission or confirmation to let go of the ledge and put yourself first to have a relationship with God, I am here to give it to you. Open your heart. *ACCESS GRANTED*!